About the Book

Birds are undoubte[...] [...] easily seen and enjoy[...] [...], first published in 1937, w[...] [...] first small book designed to enable non-experts, children and adults alike, to identify and learn about the various species. Now Rob Hume has completely rewritten the book for the paperback *Observers* series, giving comprehensive coverage of over 170 birds, those most likely to be seen in the British Isles. He describes each bird's distinctive features, behaviour, habitat, 'voice' and food, and where and how it nests and rears its young. Each entry is illustrated in full colour, the picture usually showing both sexes if their appearance differs; and the book has the distinction of providing very many classic illustrations by the celebrated bird artist Archibald Thorburn.

About the Author

Rob Hume has been interested in birds from his childhood, and in his early teens began to keep notes of his observations. His early experience was in Staffordshire, with frequent excursions to Essex and Scotland; later he travelled more widely, to extend his opportunities for birdwatching, and since 1978 he has watched birds in many other countries, including Iceland, Egypt and Zimbabwe. He spent two years carrying out field surveys (of the incidence of plants and butterflies as well as of birds) for the Royal Society for the Protection of Birds in the hills of mid Wales, before moving to the RSPB's headquarters at Sandy in 1978, where he worked in the Development Department and became an experienced lecturer. He moved to the Publications Department in 1983. He has published several papers, especially on the identification of gulls and terns, a field guide and a birdwatcher's anthology, and many magazine features on birds and birdwatching experiences. He is also an accomplished artist whose illustrations appear in a number of bird books and magazines.

The *Observer's* series was launched in 1937 with the publication of *The Observer's Book of Birds*. Today, fifty years later, paperback *Observers* continue to offer practical, useful information on a wide range of subjects, and with every book regularly revised by experts, the facts are right up-to-date. Students, amateur enthusiasts and professional organisations alike will find the latest *Observers* invaluable.

'Thick and glossy, briskly informative' – *The Guardian*

'If you are a serious spotter of any of the things the series deals with, the books must be indispensable' – *The Times Educational Supplement*

O B S E R V E R ' S

BIRDS

Rob Hume

Describing and illustrating in full colour 171 species
found in the British Isles

FREDERICK WARNE

FREDERICK WARNE
Penguin Books Ltd, Harmondsworth, Middlesex, England
Viking Penguin Inc., 40 West 23rd Street, New York, New York 10010, U.S.A.
Penguin Books Australia Ltd, Ringwood, Victoria, Australia
Penguin Books Canada Limited, 2801 John Street, Markham, Ontario, Canada L3R 1B4
Penguin Books (N.Z.) Ltd, 182–190 Wairau Road, Auckland 10, New Zealand

First published 1987
Reprinted 1989

ISBN 0 7232 1685 1

Printed and bound in Great Britain by
William Clowes Limited,
Beccles and London

CONTENTS

PREFACE

The original *Observer's Book of Birds* was written at a time when few reliable pocket books on birds in Britain were to be found. The author, S. Vere Benson, achieved a valuable compilation of information on 200 bird species, compressing details on identification, behaviour, range and status, habitat, food, calls and nest and eggs alongside the illustration on each page, and so awakening an interest in birds amongst thousands of young (or old) collectors of the famous *Observer's Book* series. It was my first comprehensive bird book and I well remember reading in its pages of birds such as the Chiffchaff and the Lesser Whitethroat, which were unknown to me as a boy and seemed to be unlikely exotics that I might never manage to glimpse!

By going out and finding some of them, and referring constantly to the little book, I gave my new-found enthusiasm more purpose and more knowledge to keep it going. The debt which I, like so many other birdwatchers, owe to the book is huge. It is, therefore, with a mixture of pride and diffidence that I have embarked upon this new revision, and I must record my debt to Miss Vere Benson. I must also thank Stephanie Mullins, who originally commissioned me to rewrite this book and helped enormously with its planning. My wife, Marcella, supplied endless encouragement and ideas during the book's preparation.

I am fortunate in the book's illustrations, which are taken from Lord Lilford's *Coloured Figures of the Birds of the British Isles* and comprise many paintings by Archibald Thorburn and other well-known bird artists of his period. These have been supplemented by the work of Robert Gillmor, who has painted the pictures on pages 30 (Canada Goose), 47 (Ruddy Duck), 109 (Collared Dove), 161 (Willow Tit), and 171 (Carrion Crow). The picture on page 172 (Raven) is by Ernest C. Mansell.

Rob Hume

INTRODUCTION

This book gives basic facts about the lives of most of the birds which the average interested, and fairly observant person is likely to see in the course of one or two years' travelling about in the British Isles. A little travel is essential, because many species can only be found in certain areas—it is no use looking for a Golden Eagle in Sussex, or a Nuthatch in Strathclyde, for example. There are, of course, many other birds which could be squeezed in; they are scarce, or restricted to small areas, but it should be borne in mind that one may always come across something not in the book. It is, however, true to say that you are much more likely to see a common bird (even if you cannot name it) than something exotic. Individual birds of a single species vary; in some, the differences are very great (for example, between summer and winter, male and female, adult and young). Where these differences are marked, I have attempted to describe them; but remember that the appearance of a bird, even of one with the most basic colour and pattern, can vary according to the light, the state of its plumage and other circumstances. The most colourful of birds may look black against the light; yet, viewed against the sun, the black of a Crow may momentarily shine silver.

Several basic problems arise in portraying a bird in words. Colours described as 'warm', or 'reddish' may seem to another observer to require quite different interpretations. It is never easy to describe size. The length of a bird, expressed here in centimetres or metres, is the distance from bill-tip to tail-tip when the bird is lying flat on its back—rarely the way we see one. So a living bird in the wild ('in the field', as birdwatchers say) will tend to be a touch shorter as it hunches up its head. In any case, the odd centimetre is rarely easy to judge or of much use in identification. But it is always essential to get at least a rough idea—is the bird in question about the size of a sparrow, or a thrush, or a crow? Accurate judgment is fraught with difficulties but such an estimate should not be too difficult. To aid comparisons, a simple subdivision has been attempted in the descriptions in this book. Birds have been put into six groups: (1) very small, or tit size (up to 12 cm); (2) small, or sparrow size (13–18 cm); (3) medium, or thrush size (19–27 cm); (4) large, or pigeon size (28–55 cm); (5) very large, or goose size (56–85 cm) and (6) huge, or the size of a heron or swan (86 cm plus).

But length alone is not an entirely satisfactory indication of size. Bulk and wing-span also affect our impression of a bird. The difference between a Lesser Black-backed Gull and a Great Black-backed Gull is only a few centimetres; but, side by side, the Great Black-back may look 'twice as big' as the Lesser. It is so much more bulky and heavily built. So, as a further indication of a bird's size, this book also includes its weight, a detail rarely given in a small guide. You will therefore be able to appreciate the difference between two birds of equal length, one of which is long, slim and lightweight, and the other tubby and heavy. Of course a bird's weight changes a lot; but the rounded figures give a rough indication.

The calls of a bird are also hard to put onto paper. I often think that words such as 'twink' or 'chereep' only help if you already know the call, and serve to bring it back to mind; but at least they are better than nothing, and bird calls and songs are valuable in identification. If you go out with an experienced birdwatcher, you will find that he or she picks up most birds on call. The best way to learn the calls yourself is through having such a friend, or by going out on a club's field trips. The only way, really, to take everything in is to spend hours outside listening and looking.

The book is unable to present maps of distribution. Remember to check comments in the text; and remember that some birds are found only in the south, or north, or, say, in the southwest. Some may be seen in the summer but not in winter; others in spring and autumn; others only in the winter, or perhaps mainly in the winter with a few lingering through the summer months. The text gives these details, which must always be checked as well as the pictures.

The letters **R**, **S**, **W** and **M** have been used to give the following broad indications: **R** for resident species (seen all the year round); **S** for summer visitors (in reality arriving in March or April and often staying until

September or October); **W** for winter visitors (likewise spread from autumn to spring); and **M** for migrants, which neither spend the summer here nor stay for the winter, but are seen en route from breeding grounds in the north to wintering grounds in the south each autumn, and on the way back each spring. Spring and autumn are times of great movements in the bird world, and consequently of much excitement for the birdwatcher. But these letters may be misleading locally; for instance, Curlews and Meadow Pipits spend the summer on high hills and moors and the winter on the coast—so they are residents, here all year round, but not necessarily in the same spot.

The true residents—such as Nuthatch or Dunnock—may hardly move out of their regular territory all year round. Some summer visitors appear in the winter as well, but in very small numbers: our breeding Blackcaps and Chiffchaffs move south, but others from further north spend the winter here. But they are the exceptions: you will not see a Swallow in January or a Swift in December—they simply would not survive. But you may be more likely to see the odd winter visitor lingering in the summer, especially if it is a duck or wader—a few of these are difficult to classify. Waders may still be moving north to their breeding grounds in the Arctic in June—only then will the snow have melted—yet others may be returning south by the beginning of July! These specific details are given not in order to confuse you, but simply to make it clear that the 'status' category into which a bird is placed applies as a general guide but is not an infallible rule.

The birds are presented in the currently accepted scientific order, which seeks to start with the most primitive species and progress to the most recently evolved, or advanced, ones. Close relatives are therefore to be found together, which means that all warblers come in one group and all tits in another. This leaves a few similar-looking birds separated by many pages—for example, both grebes and ducks swim on water, but in the book are quite separate. There are arguments for putting them together and distorting the 'natural' sequence to aid comparison, but I have felt it better to use the scientific sequence right from the start. All serious books follow it and it is as well to gain familiarity through use; and it is also a help to realise that grebes are *not* ducks, and herons are *not* waders. Then their differences in structure, pattern and way of life become more obvious and are easier to understand. The systematic order, as it is called, is a source of interest and enlightenment in itself.

How should I watch birds?

First, it is almost essential to get a good pair of binoculars. Get as good a pair as you can afford, with a well-known name; one that is light, easy to use and comfortable. You will have to balance the advantages of large lenses (which give a bright image), small size (and therefore lightness of weight) and large magnification (which means a smaller field of view and less close focussing). It is not possible to have everything! Go for 7 × 50, 8 × 30, 8 × 40, 10 × 40 or 10 × 50. The first figure is the magnification; the second is the diameter in millimetres of the large lenses (the bigger they are the more light they let in). A magnification of more than 10 is too great for general use; don't be tempted by some monster pair, which will prove quite unmanageable.

Secondly, get a notebook and use it. Keep a diary and take notes of what you see. You may simply keep lists at first (and then more selective notes of species seen). If you see something unusual, or new to you, take a description of it—practise on common birds (even on photographs) if you like, until you can do it more thoroughly. Learn which bit of a bird is which (see the diagram on page 14) so that you can write the description down accurately (it is hopelessly vague to talk of 'a bit of brown on top' and 'a patch of colour underneath'). Try to write down the basic colours, then fill in the details of bill and legs, any pattern which catches the eye such as a bar on the wing or a stripe over the eye, and remember the bird's shape, size and behaviour, and the date and place where it was seen. It sounds a lot to do, and is not easy at first, but is a good deal of fun and really sharpens up your observation. But it is the fun that matters—after all, you will be watching birds because you enjoy it, not to pass an exam. The important thing to remember is that doing it right to begin with—taking notes, learning your birds, reading books—all adds to the enjoyment. If you start off on the wrong track, especially if there is no knowledgeable friend to put you right, it may take years to get back on the right course.

You will profit by first watching birds in a garden or park. Then explore further afield, looking at different types of habitat—woodland, the local river, or a lake or gravel-pit. You will soon find that water and waterside places add greatly to the variety of birds you will see. If you find a productive spot near home—a particular wood, or pool, or weedy field—it is often a good thing to look upon it as your local patch and visit it regularly, every week if you can. By doing so you will get to know it and the birds there, and enjoy the new and unexpected more than ever. You might even become the local expert!

But it is also all to the good if you travel about a bit. That is the only way to see a greater variety of birds and to broaden your knowledge and experience. Some people say they never travel in search of birds but are content to see what comes to them. But if you live in a town you will never see wildfowl and waders, or if you are in farmland in the middle of England you will never see seabirds; so travel if you can, and enjoy what you can find.

Join a bird club or the local group of the Royal Society for the Protection of Birds (or Young Ornithologists' Club if you are under 15). With them you can go out with other beginners and a few experts, too, which is a good way to learn and to make friends.

Do your 'homework' too! It is a good idea to spend the winter reading about the summer birds, ready for their arrival in spring—then they won't be so confusing! Books are unbeatable for learning and the more you read, the more you will know. Get a more advanced field guide when you are ready; read books on single species or groups, or habitats, read magazines, watch the television. There is now more help available to the birdwatcher than ever before, so take advantage of it; you can become as good a birdwatcher in a few years as past generations were in a lifetime. But that is not to say that you can ever become a real expert without years of experience—get out and watch the birds whenever you can. If you only go on holiday once or twice a year and put up the binoculars and books in the meantime, you can't expect to identify things, any more than a top-class sportsman, or musician, can expect to give perfect performances without hours of practice behind the scenes.

Birds in the garden

You can encourage birds to come to you by putting out food and water. A bird-table is a tidy way of doing it, but some birds prefer to feed on the ground. Try to give a variety of food—bread and kitchen scraps, grain and sunflower seeds on the table for finches, robins and thrushes; peanuts in a hanging basket or plastic mesh bag for tits and Greenfinches; rotten apples, wild bird seed, kitchen scraps on the ground for Blackbirds, Dunnocks and Starlings. Most food will be suitable, but *do* remember to cut up bacon rinds, and *don't* put out dried foods such as dessicated coconut, which are harmful to birds. Information is available from the RSPB if you send a stamped addressed envelope.

Feed them only from late autumn to early spring. Artificial food is dangerous for young birds. In any case, it is unfair to tempt birds to nest by supplying artificial food which may be withdrawn if you go away for a weekend or on holiday; if there is not enough natural food available, the birds should not be nesting there. Anyway, they do more good in the spring by eating caterpillars than by eating your nuts!

You can build a bird-box to encourage tits and other species to nest. Details are available from the RSPB (or ready-made boxes can be bought from them).

If you find a 'lost' young bird *please leave it alone*. Its parents will be watching nearby. They can feed it; you will not be able to. If you 'rescue' a young bird and take it home, it will surely die. If it is in danger from a cat, or in the middle of a road, move it gently to a safe place, where its parents will be able to find it.

Birds and the law

All wild birds and their eggs are protected by law. A very few species may be killed by landowners on their own land, or by people they specifically authorize, and in a very few cases a landowner may, with a special licence, kill a bird if it is causing damage to crops and no other remedy is available. But no-one may kill even an unprotected bird on public land, or on private land without the owner's permission; and even a landowner on his own ground may not kill a protected species. Rarer species are especially protected, and there are extra severe penalties for damaging them; you may not even visit their nests without a licence. So the best thing is to consider all birds, all eggs and all nests protected by law, everywhere.

Clubs to join

Join the local (often county-based) bird club, or natural history society. The biggest national organization concerned with protecting birds is the Royal Society for the Protection of Birds, at The Lodge, Sandy, Bedfordshire, SG19 2DL. It has more than 400,000 members and runs more than 100 reserves; as a member you get a big, colourful magazine four times a year. Junior members (under 15) join the Young Ornithologists' Club, over 85,000 strong, with its own magazine appearing every two months. The address is the same.

Books to read

The Birdwatcher's Yearbook, edited by John E. Pemberton (Buckingham Press), is an annual paperback, giving details of other clubs to join, with more specialized aims, including ringing and census schemes, and local or national surveys. It also gives details of people to contact if you wish to report the birds you see (a good idea), and lists hundreds of places to visit.

The Birdlife of Britain, by Peter Hayman and Philip Burton (Mitchell Beazley, 1976), is an excellent guide.

The Mitchell Beazley Birdwatcher's Pocket Guide, by Peter Hayman (1979), is a comprehensive field guide.

The RSPB Book of British Birds, by Peter Holden, J. T. R. Sharrock and Hilary Burn (Macmillan, 1982).

A Field Guide to the Birds of Britain and Europe, by Roger Peterson, Guy Mountfort and P. A. D. Hollom (Collins, 4th Edition, 1983).

Shorebirds: a Guide to the Waders of the World, by Peter Hayman, John Marchant and Tony Prater (Croom Helm, 1986).

Birds in Scotland, by Valerie Thom (Poyser, 1986).

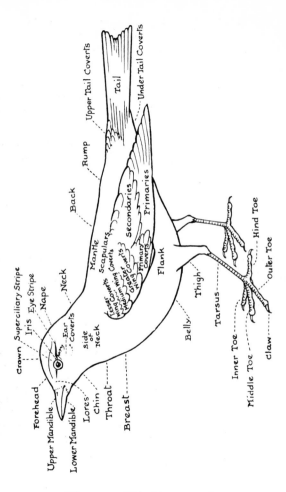

Diagram of bird topography

NOTE ON THE ARRANGEMENT
OF THE ENTRIES

The name of the bird (one particular species) is given in English, and is followed by the scientific name (based on Greek or Latin) in italics. The first word of the scientific name gives the genus to which the bird belongs and shows which species are closely related; the second word indicates the species. The two words together always name one species of bird only.

The bird's length is given in centimetres (or metres) and its **weight** in grammes (or kilogrammes). Its **size group** (see page 7) is indicated by a number:

1   very small (up to 12 cm)
2   small (13–18 cm)
3   medium (19–27 cm)
4   large (28–55 cm)
5   very large (56–85 cm)
6   huge (86 cm plus)

The bird's 'status' (the time of year when it is likely to be seen—see page 8) is indicated by a letter:

R   resident
S   summer visitor
W   winter visitor
M   migrant

The main text gives hints on identification and behaviour. These are followed by details of: **habitat** (the kind of country in which the bird is found); **nest** (if the bird breeds in the British Isles), together with information about eggs, incubation period and the time the young spend in the nest before they can fly; **food**; and **voice**. Where calls have been written down (*hooeet*, for example), it is the hope that the letters will give an approximate idea of the sound; phrases such as 'shrill and sharp', 'liquid whistle', 'rapid twitter', etc, are inevitably vague. A hyphen between syllables is meant to indicate speed; for example, *chew-chew-chew* would be a quicker call than *chew chew chew*.

Little Grebe
Tachybaptus ruficollis

Length: 26 cm
3

Weight: 100–290 g
R

A small, round, tail-less bird that swims and dives in rivers and small, sheltered lakes, especially where there is vegetation on the bank. In summer it is a dark bird with red-brown on the face and a bright yellowish spot at the base of the short bill. In winter it is browner, with a paler face, and is buffish, not white, beneath. It is not often seen in flight, but usually only skittering across the water for a few yards, when its outstretched head and trailing legs make it look longer. Very young birds have dark stripes on the head, but they soon become dull brown and buff, like the adults in winter. **Habitat** still and slow-moving water, including rivers, canals, lakes and reservoirs and even park ponds, with some shoreline vegetation. Some visit sheltered sea coasts in winter. **Nest** amongst emergent vegetation or beneath overhanging branches in which it can anchor a mound of water-weed. It lays 4–6 dull whitish eggs, which it covers when it leaves the nest. Widespread except in northern Scotland. **Food** mainly small fish, aquatic insects and molluscs. **Voice** includes a distinctive high, whinnying trill.

Great Crested Grebe

Podiceps cristatus

Length: 48 cm

Weight: 600–1400 g

4

R

A slim, elegant water bird to be seen swimming on open water, often sliding underneath in search of fish. It is not now rare, but suitable haunts are naturally restricted. The glistening white neck and breast always catch the eye, although the neck may be withdrawn. In winter it is otherwise dull, grey-brown above and white below, with a black cap and eyestripe; the pointed bill is distinctive. Summer plumage includes a striking, broad, chestnut and black frill each side of the head, and black tufts on the nape; the flanks are more rufous. It has lobed toes instead of webbed feet, but it is far more restricted to water than are ducks. It is not often seen in flight, and almost never on land. **Habitat** lakes and reservoirs of all kinds, but for nesting it requires vegetation at the edge and a good supply of fish; it is also found on broad rivers, and on the sea, especially in winter. **Nest** amongst reeds or flooded willows, where it lays 3–4 white eggs on a bed of floating weed. The young have striped heads and are fed by the adults for several weeks. Rarely found breeding in the north and west. **Food** predominantly fish. **Voice** includes a variety of loud, throaty growls in summer; the young whistle loudly.

Fulmar

Fulmarus glacialis

Length: 47 cm

Weight: 600–1100 g

4

R

This grey and white seabird is most often to be seen gliding along sea cliffs or flying low over the open sea. Superficially gull-like, it is easily distinguished in flight by its narrow, rather straight and stiff wings, which are grey above, often with brownish smudges and a paler area near the tip, but without any black. The head and neck are white, tinged with yellow, and protrude as a large white patch visible at long range, whereas the tail, unlike those of gulls, is grey. When seen on land, its large, dark eye and thick, hook-tipped bill with tubular nostrils also distinguish it. Fulmars are at home in the roughest weather, flying like small albatrosses above the waves, banking from side to side in the wind; but in calm weather they fly low and direct with fast wingbeats. **Habitat** the sea; comes to land only to breed, but does visit colonies during the winter. **Nest** on ledges of cliffs and steep grassy slopes above the sea, often scattered above the denser colonies of other seabirds that nest on the more vertical rock faces. Usually lays just one large, white egg which is incubated for eight weeks; the young bird does not fly until eight weeks old and will not breed for several years. Widespread around coasts wherever cliffs are available. **Food** largely fish, crustacea, offal from trawlers. **Voice** at the nest, a loud raucous cackling.

Manx Shearwater

Puffinus puffinus

Length: 35 cm

Weight: 340–500 g

4

S

Few birds have more romantic appeal than the Manx Shearwater, which lives far out at sea and comes to land only to nest, and only then under the safe cover of darkness. Shearwaters can be seen in the daytime from headlands around our coasts, especially in the west, flying low over the sea, flapping rapidly for a few seconds and then gliding, their wings stiff and straight, tilting over from side to side to ride the air currents over the waves. They look slender and long-winged, black above and gleaming white beneath. In rough weather they rise high above the water in steep, banking glides. At dusk they gather offshore, ready to visit the colony. **Habitat** the open sea, occasionally in more enclosed bays and estuaries, especially if driven by storms. **Nest** in colonies on islands, sometimes high on barren mountain tops, in burrows or cavities amongst boulders. One egg is laid in spring and adults take turns of 7–10 days' incubation, without food, for a total of 51–54 days. The young fly when over 70 days old, having been abandoned by the parents after about 60 days. **Food** fish. **Voice** at the colonies, loud and weird; in flight and from the burrows, rapid, strangled crowing noises made by thousands together.

Gannet

Sula bassana

Length: 90 cm

Weight: 2·5–3·5 kg

6

R

Our largest seabird, with a wing-span approaching 1·8 m, the Gannet is majestic and handsome in the air. Adults are white, except for black wing-tips and a yellow area on the head; compared with grey-backed gulls they look gleaming white, even at a great distance. Immatures are largely blackish, with white speckling, and birds at intermediate stages are patchy above, white below. In flight, as they are usually seen unless at a breeding colony, they look long and slender, with head and neck protruding and a pointed tail. The flight is powerful and direct, with regular beats of the long, pointed wings; but in strong winds the Gannet is an accomplished glider. **Habitat** the sea; some may be seen in sheltered inshore waters, sometimes swimming buoyantly. **Nest** in large colonies, typically of several thousand pairs, on steep cliffs of rocky islands in the north and west; there is one mainland colony in Yorkshire. One egg is laid, and incubated for 43–45 days. **Food** fish, caught by plunge-diving from the air, often from low altitude but also, most spectacularly, in a headlong plunge ending in a huge splash. **Voice** at the colony, a loud, hoarse *urrah* that, coming from thousands of throats, makes a rhythmic continuous chorus.

Cormorant
Phalacrocorax carbo

Length: 90 cm
6

Weight: 2–2·8 kg
R

A large, dark water bird, distinctive in flight and on the water, or when perched, as it often is, on a buoy, jetty or tree. It has a long body but very short legs, a broad tail longer than that of any goose, and a moderately long neck. The thick, hook-tipped bill gives a heavier appearance to the head than is the case with the Shag, the only really similar species. In flight the head is extended, the wings long but blunt, and the action rather goose-like. On the water, it swims very low, with head and neck erect and bill uptilted; it is a skilful diver. When perched it may adopt a slanting pose with wings outstretched as if to dry. Adults are all very dark except for a white face patch and white thigh patches in spring; immatures are browner above and white below. **Habitat** coastal waters, including muddy estuaries and sandy bays, as well as rockier shores. Frequent inland, both on large lakes and reservoirs and on broad rivers, beside which there may be regularly used treetop perches 'whitewashed' with droppings. **Nest** on cliffs in colonies, much more rarely inland in trees. Lays 3–4 eggs in a bulky nest of seaweed, sticks and grass. **Food** very largely fish. **Voice** includes deep, throaty noises, mostly at nest and roost sites.

Shag

Phalacrocorax aristotelis

Length: 75 cm
5
Weight: 1·5–2·2 kg
R

Compared with the Cor-
morant this is a more
slender bird, with a much
less heavy head and bill,
and it is much more
restricted to the sea. It is especially at home on the rocky
coasts of the north and west, swimming and diving with
ease in the roughest sea. Otherwise it is much like a
Cormorant, but greener overall, lacking the white on the
face (but it does have a prominent yellow chin) and on the
thighs. In spring adults have a short, upcurved crest.
Young birds are brown, darker beneath than young
Cormorants, having white on the throat only, but they are
best identified by their lighter build. The shag often leaps
forward clear of the water as it dives. **Habitat** inshore
waters near wild, rocky coasts with steep cliffs and dark,
deep caves or jumbled boulders; very rare inland.
Nest on cliff ledges or in deep fissures, often in large
colonies betrayed by vast areas of white droppings. Lays
2–3 eggs in a bulky structure of heather stalks, seaweed
and grasses. **Food** almost entirely fish, pursued underwater after a dive from the surface. **Voice** harsh and
croaking, especially in defence of the nest.

Grey Heron
Ardea cinerea

Length: 90 cm
6

Weight: 1·1–1·75 kg
R

No other common bird should be mistaken for the tall, sombre Grey Heron, a quiet, patient fisherman stalking the edges of any water, from the smallest pool or ditch to the largest lake, and even the sea coast. Herons also often stand in fields and perch freely in trees, but their grey plumage, long legs and long (but often curved into an S-shape) necks make them hard to mistake. Adults have white heads and necks, with a black stripe over the eye continuing into a thin crest, and black streaks on the foreneck. Young birds are generally duller and greyer overall. In spring the adult may develop a brightly coloured bill, usually yellow, but sometimes more pink or orange. In flight the huge size and very broad, rounded, arched wings are highly distinctive; the head is withdrawn onto the shoulders. **Habitat** water's edge of any kind, from riversides in arable areas to rocky, seaweed-covered shore. **Nest** in treetop colonies, sometimes in lower scrub or even on the ground where trees are absent; very widespread, but colonies thinly scattered. Lays 3–5 eggs in a large nest of sticks. Young leave the nest at 50–55 days old. **Food** largely fish, particularly eels, but all sorts may be taken; also frogs, water voles, young birds. **Voice** a very distinctive loud, sharp *frarnk*, and many loud and raucous noises at the nest.

Mute Swan

Cygnus olor

Length: 1·5 m

Weight: 8–14 kg

6

R

Huge, familiar and popular, Mute Swans have declined greatly in many areas in recent years, very largely as a result of accidental poisoning by lead spilt by anglers and spread from widespread shooting. They are an important feature of the English scene—though equally at-home on remote Scottish coastal lochs—and deserve our best protection. The frequently-curved neck, and especially the downward tilt to the head, the cocked, pointed tail and the distinctive bill distinguish the Mute from other swans. Adults have orange bills with black at the tip and base, with a black basal knob. Young birds, brown at first and quickly becoming patchy, have a similar bill pattern in black and grey, but lack the knob. **Habitat** based on still or slow-flowing water, mostly fresh, where there is vegetation on the bank or in shallow water. **Nest** near water or in emergent vegetation; it lays 5–7 large eggs in a huge pile of leaves, stems and roots. Frequently vandalized. Both sexes incubate, for five weeks, and the young fly after 4½ months. **Food** largely underwater vegetation, taken by submerging head and neck or upending to reach greater depth. **Voice** a variety of strangled and snorting noises and hisses. In flight the wings make a rhythmic, humming throb.

Whooper Swan

Cygnus cygnus

Length: 1·5 m

Weight: 8–10 kg

W

This bird is very similar to the **Bewick's Swan** (*C. columbianus*, 1·2 m long and weighing 5–7 kg); both are pure white swans (greyer in juvenile plumage) that visit Britain only in winter and behave in a very much wilder fashion than the common Mute Swan. They lack its bill knob, pointed tail, frequently arched wings and throbbing wingbeats, and look stiffer-necked, even on dry land. The Whooper has a longer, flatter bill and head profile than the Bewick's, and the basal yellow area on its beak extends further forward into a point on each side. Bewick's Swan is rounder-headed, shorter-billed, and has a smaller, rounder area of yellow (often divided by a central black stripe). **Habitat** Bewick's Swans, locally the more numerous, occur on floods and water-meadows (mostly on reserves) in the south and east; Whoopers may overlap with them, but mainly visit wild lakes and wide river valleys in the north and west. **Food** vegetable matter, including grass, seeds, root crops, taken from shallows, pastures and agricultural land. **Voice** both have loud, far-carrying, ringing calls. The voice of the Bewick's is the more musical, and from flocks can develop into a quieter bubbling babble; the Whooper's is more bugling in quality, *ahng* or *whoop*.

Pink-footed Goose
Anser brachyrhynchus

Length: 75 cm

5

Weight: 2–3 kg

W

Perhaps the most attractive of the grey geese, and, in the north of England and in Scotland, also the most numerous, the Pink-foot is more blue-grey above, brighter buff on the chest and more contrastingly dark on the head than are the others. It has a round, neat head and a short bill, which looks very dark but has a pink band; its legs are pink. In flight the forewings are greyer than on a White-front, but not so striking as those of a Greylag. The rare **Bean Goose** (*A. fabalis*) is closely related and very similar, but has a longer neck and head profile, a darker back and orange legs. Pink-feet may gather in flocks of several thousands and add immense interest to the winter scene in places fortunate enough to have them; but farmers may not welcome them so readily! **Habitat** agricultural land, with stubble, root and cornfields. It roosts on large, undisturbed lochs and coastal marshes, where it is wild and easily disturbed. Purely a winter visitor. **Food** includes grain from stubbles, potatoes and carrots left after harvesting, grasses. **Voice** less deep than Greylag's but not so laughing in quality as White-front's. Includes loud *ahng-ung* notes, and higher-pitched *wink-wink* calls which are particularly distinctive.

White-fronted Goose

Anser albifrons

Length: 75 cm

Weight: 2–3 kg

5

W

A darker bird than a Greylag, the adult White-front is distinctive in its white forehead blaze and broad bars of black on the under parts; it also has rich orange legs (but colours are not always easy to see!). Birds from Russia—mostly seen in a few southern localities in Britain—have pink bills, but those from Greenland—in a few places in the west and in Ireland in winter—have orange ones. Immatures lack the white and the black bars, but their bills and legs are coloured as in adults; they have an overall uniform grey-brown look, with greyer but not paler forewings, a lighter build than a Greylag but a coarser, larger-billed appearance than a Pink-foot. Geese are, however, notoriously difficult to identify in less than ideal conditions, especially in unexpected places. In huge, noisy skeins they are, nevertheless, unequalled as a spectacle in Britain. **Habitat** largely grassy marshes, salt-marshes and green fields, close to safe coastal roosts. **Food** largely grasses. **Voice** higher pitched than in most geese, with a lighter, laughing quality which makes it all the more attractive. Usually two or three syllables—*kow-yow*, *kyow-lyo-lok*, etc.

Greylag Goose

Anser anser

Length: 80 cm

Weight: 3–4 kg

5

W/R

Many Greylag Geese are now feral in southern Britain, from which the truly wild stock has long since been absent. Winter visitors in the north are really wild and far less approachable; a few native breeding birds still persist in the far northwest. They are heavy and solidly built, but still far more agile than their farmhouse descendants, both in fast, spectacular flight and when grazing on fields and marshes. Other wild geese are of slimmer build, and have darker heads and darker forewings, which are strikingly pale grey on the Greylag. The Greylag has pink legs and a very stout orange bill. **Habitat** marshland, both salt and fresh, and damp grasslands near the coast; also stubble and grain within reach of night-time roosts on large lakes or on the coast. **Nest** in heather on islands in wild areas of moor and lochs; feral birds beside gravel-pits and pools. **Food** largely grasses; also grain. **Voice** loud and far-carrying, especially from flying flocks. Much like that of domestic geese, with a rattling, cackling quality—*aahng-ung-ung.*

Canada Goose

Branta canadensis

Length: 1 m

Weight: 3–4 kg

6

R

Introduced as an ornamental waterfowl, this large goose has found much of Britain to its liking. In many regions it is the only goose likely to be seen, especially in summer, except where Greylags have also been introduced; but escaped geese of all kinds tend to associate with the flocks. For these reasons it is often dismissed by birdwatchers as unworthy of serious attention, but it is fascinating and attractive nonetheless. The black head and neck with a broad white chin-strap forms a unique feature, which makes all Canada Geese, at any age and season, very easy to pick out. They are also very large and particularly long-necked among geese. **Habitat** now varied—ornamental lakes in parkland and estates, town parks, gravel-pits, reservoirs, even large rivers. **Nest** on the ground, often on an island, beside a pool or flooded pit. Lays 5–6 large white eggs; goslings hatch after 28–29 days and are fully grown after six weeks. **Food** largely grass. **Voice** a deep, resonant honking—*ah-honk*.

Brent Goose

Branta bernicla

Length: 58 cm

Weight: 1·2–1·4 kg

5

W

On the coasts of east and southern England this is now a commonly found goose in winter on suitably muddy shores, and on adjacent marshes and fields in years when the numbers are high. These are dark-bellied birds, but a paler-bellied race also occurs in the northeast and in Ireland. Although not much bigger than a Mallard, its shape and actions are much more typical of a goose than of a duck, and, on the wing especially, its size is deceptive. It has long, broad, pointed wings, a thick neck and short tail, and its flight is strong and rapid. The black head, neck and breast, dark wings and back and striking white stern make it an easy goose to identify; adults have a white mark on the neck, but juveniles lack this at first and show pale bars across the wing coverts. **Habitat** coastal; it frequents muddy flats and estuaries, often swimming on the sea. **Food** vegetable matter from the intertidal zone and increasingly from salt-marshes and from pastures or fields of young corn. Provision of grassy refuge areas would reduce conflict with farmers. **Voice** deep and throaty, a single, rough syllable—*krronk*.

Shelduck

Tadorna tadorna

Length: 60 cm

Weight: 950–1400 g

5

R

More goose-like in bearing than other ducks, the Shelduck is unmistakable in its piebald plumage, set off by pink legs and a deep red bill. Males have a large red knob at the base of the bill, absent on females, which often have whitish areas on the face and cheek. Young birds are recognizable by their shape and size, but lack the broad band of chestnut around the body which is so obvious on their parents, and have the dark areas browner and the face largely white. Shelducks feed on mud and in marshy areas, walking slowly on long legs, but they also upend in the shallows. They are common on much of the lower-lying coastal areas of Britain. **Habitat** both muddy and sandy estuaries; it is also not rare inland, where a few pairs breed. Most prefer coastal dunes and areas of rough grazing near the shore in which to nest. **Nest** in a rabbit hole or similar burrow, or under brambles; it lays 8–15 creamy eggs in May. The female incubates for four weeks, but both parents tend the young; several families may unite into large crèches. **Food** largely tiny marine snails and similar animal matter sieved from mud through the stout bill. **Voice** includes a nasal, quick *ah-ah-ah-ah*, and quiet whistling notes.

Wigeon
Anas penelope

Length: 45 cm

Weight: 550–1000 g

4

W

A medium-sized duck, most characteristically seen in large, dense packs grazing on grass near rivers, coastal marshes or large reservoirs. The Wigeon is locally abundant in winter, but is rare as a breeding bird. Somewhat like a Teal in pattern, the drake shows a different contrast between dark head and pale body, while the Wigeon duck is generally more rufous. Drakes have a large white patch on the forewing, most obvious in flight, whereas the duck simply has a rather greyer patch. The yellow forehead of the male is often striking in good light. In flight both sexes show pointed tails and long, slim wings, but short, round heads. **Habitat** lakes in moorland areas in the north of Britain hold a few breeding pairs. Outside the breeding season, on salt-marshes, water-meadows and grassy reservoir shores. **Nest** on ground, containing 7–8 creamy eggs. **Food** very largely grasses and salt-marsh vegetation, mostly taken by birds walking steadily forward in close flocks. **Voice** of the duck is a distinctive low growl. The drake has a bright, loud whistle, a musical note suited to its wild marshland habitat—*whee-oo*.

Gadwall

Anas strepera

Length: 50 cm

Weight: 600–1300 g

4

R

Once very local and scarce, the Gadwall is now much more numerous, especially in the east of England, largely due to introductions. The drake is a greyer bird than most surface-feeding ducks, with a paler, browner head and, most noticeably, a black stern with no white on it. The pale orange-yellow legs may be conspicuous. The ducks are mottled brown, with a rather paler, rounded head and a smaller bill than that of a Mallard. Both ducks and drakes have a square white patch near the base of the wing, often hidden at rest but obvious in flight. In flight their shape is closer to that of a Mallard than to the dumpier, sharp-tailed Wigeon. **Habitat** still waters, especially secluded lakes, pools and backwaters with plenty of thick cover on the banks; in winter occupies more open lakes and reservoirs and sometimes coastal marshes. **Nest** on the ground in thick vegetation close to water. It lays 8–12 creamy eggs, which are incubated by the duck for 27–28 days. **Food** mostly vegetable, especially buds, seeds and succulent stems of aquatic plants. **Voice** is distinctive, especially the deep, nasal quack of the drake—a short *nhek*; the duck has a quiet quack.

Teal

Anas crecca

Length: 21 cm

3

Weight: 200–430 g

R

Small, agile, swift in flight and quick off the mark when disturbed, the Teal is a dark, compact duck whose intricate pattern is seen well only at close range. It is smaller than the Wigeon and looks darker, the drake being dark grey with a brown and green head, a horizontal white line along the body and a triangle of yellow in front of the tail. The duck is mottled brown, much as in several other species, but like the drake has a patch of vivid green, edged with white, on the wing. Both have grey legs and bills. **Habitat** bogs and small pools on moors in the summer; otherwise lakes, reservoirs, flooded gravel-pits and all sorts of marshy areas, including salt-marshes. **Nest** on ground near marsh or pool; lays 8–10 buffish or greenish eggs. Only the duck incubates, for three weeks, but the drake may help to tend the young. **Food** largely water weeds and seeds of aquatic plants, taken from mud, waterside vegetation and shallows. **Voice** is often difficult to pin down, but clearly characteristic once it has been learnt—a far-carrying, musical whistle-like *krik krik* from the drake; the duck quacks.

Mallard
Anas platyrhynchos

Length: 58 cm
5

Weight: 800–1500 g
R

This is the familiar duck of the park ponds, and is often very tame. Nevertheless, the Mallard is a truly wild bird and may often be very wary. The drakes are easily identified, except in late summer when they moult into a dull plumage, called the 'eclipse'; their bright colours are then temporarily absent. In full plumage they have gorgeous bottle-green heads above a white collar, brown breasts and grey bodies with lengthwise bands of brown. The stern is black, with curly black feathers above the white tail. Females are much browner, mottled and streaked; but they have whitish tails and, like the drakes, a broad patch of violet, edged white, on the hindwing. Both sexes have vivid orange legs. The drake has a yellowish bill, even in his dull brown 'eclipse'; that of the duck is patched with orange on olive-brown. **Habitat** water and waterside areas of all sorts, fresh and salt. Often feeds on open fields as well as marshes. **Nest** in fairly thick cover near water; nest lined with grass, leaves, feathers and down, well-hidden. Lays 7–16 grey-green eggs. Widespread. **Food** mostly vegetable—seeds, roots, grasses and grain. Feeds in shallow water, often upending, and on land. **Voice** includes the familiar loud quack, from females.

Pintail
Anas acuta

Length: 55 cm
4

Weight: 600–1100 g
W

Amongst its elegant relatives the Pintail stands out as most slender and graceful of all, be it the long-tailed drake or the duller, shorter-tailed duck. Even the female has a long, slender neck, slim bill and pointed tail, especially evident when alarmed or in flight. In the air a narrow stripe of white along the trailing edge of the wing identifies her; on the ground the grey legs and bill and pale greyish head and neck distinguish her from the duck Mallard. The drake has a satin white breast continuing as a stripe up the side of the brown head; the body is grey, with a touch of yellow in front of the black and white stern. **Habitat** mostly coastal marshes, but also large lakes and reservoirs and inland floods. **Nest** on islands of lakes or in low vegetation near water; a rare breeding bird in Britain. **Food** mostly grasses, seeds and roots, but also molluscs and worms, taken in shallow water or while grazing on the marsh, often at night. Feeding flocks may be large in a few places, but usually small numbers scattered amongst the commoner wildfowl. **Voice** hardly heard.

Shoveler

Anas clypeata

Length: 50 cm

Weight: 600–900 g

4

R

One of the larger, heavier ducks, typically swimming low in the water and tipped forward, the shoulders almost awash and the bill half submerged. The long, broad bill is usually very evident, but the female may look not unlike a duck Mallard (whose bill is quite heavy, too). However, its shorter neck and smaller size help distinguish the Shoveler—in flight the long heavy head and pale, bright bluish forewings also make it look quite different from the Mallard. Drakes have even brighter blue wing patches; in their 'eclipse', which is long-lasting, they are dark and mottled, with dark heads and much rufous on the flanks. In full plumage the black head, white breast and dark red-brown flanks look very handsome. **Habitat** shallow water, muddy shorelines or areas of floating weed; less often coastal marshes. **Nest** on dry ground amongst grass or reeds, even gorse or heather; 8–12 greenish eggs are incubated by the duck for 23–25 days; the young fly after about six weeks. **Food** largely vegetable but also some animal matter, taken by sieving water through the bill in typical dabbling action. **Voice** a low quack. Note that the wings make a loud noise in flight.

Pochard

Aythya ferina

Length: 45 cm

Weight: 600–1200 g

4

R

Often mingling with Tufted Ducks, Pochards are mostly nocturnal feeders and spend the day asleep, drifting in the middle of a lake or reservoir. The drakes are strikingly pale grey, black at each end, with a rich red-brown head and scarlet eyes. With bright light on them, they look very smart indeed. The ducks are duller and browner, with a hint of the same pattern, but have brownish heads with a pale area on the chin and face. In flight all show a grey wing-bar and lack white. Drakes have a less distinct 'eclipse' than most wildfowl, and are simply a little duller in summer. **Habitat** the small breeding population prefers sheltered lakes and pools surrounded by reeds and similar dense vegetation; otherwise they are found on open water, usually fresh. **Nest** closer to water than those of most other ducks, even built up in water amongst vegetation. Lays 6–11 eggs, which are incubated for 24–28 days. **Food** largely vegetable matter (unlike that of the Tufted Duck), taken underwater after a surface dive. **Voice** rarely heard—drakes in summer have a wheezing *ah-oo*.

Tufted Duck
Aythya fuligula

Length: 42 cm
4

Weight: 350–950 g
R

This is our most familiar diving duck, active by day in small groups or larger flocks, diving for food at frequent intervals. The drakes are strikingly black-and-white except in summer 'eclipse'; their white sides and the drooping black crest easily identify them. The ducks are much browner, with only slightly paler flanks—they are darker than Pochards. Some have whitish patches near the bill and under the tail. Both sexes have yellow eyes and show a white wing-stripe in flight. The Tufted Duck is rounder in shape than other diving ducks and swims high on the water, very buoyantly. **Habitat** fresh water, usually open; often large reservoirs and flooded gravel-pits. **Nest** beside the more sheltered and undisturbed waters, on the ground within a few metres of water. The duck lays 6–14 grey-green eggs and incubates them for 23–26 days. The young leave the nest very quickly and follow the duck, diving from an early stage. They fly after six or seven weeks. **Food** mostly animal matter—frogs, insects, molluscs and the like, taken underwater. **Voice** includes a deep growl from the duck, and low rapid whistles from displaying drakes.

Scaup
Aythya marila

Length: 47 cm
4

Weight: 850–1300 g
W

A well-proportioned, large and heavy diving duck, in some ways looking intermediate between the Tufted Duck and Pochard. Unlike the Tufted, the drake has a pale grey back, and it differs from the Pochard in having white flanks and a black head, with bright yellow eyes. Ducks are more difficult to identify; they are like large pale Tufteds but with a rounder head, often a pale patch on the ear coverts, and a broader blaze of white around the bill. Young birds are similar but with less white—they have grey bills with just a tiny black spot at the tip (larger in Tufteds and Pochards). All show a long white stripe on the wing in flight. **Habitat** usually seen in winter on the sea; only rarely inland. Widely distributed, especially in the north and east; does not breed here. **Food** mostly molluscs and crustacea taken underwater after a dive from the surface. **Voice** rarely heard, but females have a deep *karr-karr-karr*.

Eider

Somateria mollissima

Length: 58 cm

Weight: 1·9–2·8 kg

5

R

This large, heavily-built maritime duck floats like a cork despite its bulk, bobbing around weed-covered rocks or drifting on the open sea well offshore. It comes to land more than most sea ducks, often in large parties, and in many areas it is quite tame. The drakes are incredibly smart and clean-cut in black, white, pink and green, but immatures are piebald. Ducks are rich brown and closely barred all over, quite unlike any other common duck. Even when distance or poor light makes the colours hard to see, the shape. with short, cocked tail, and big head with a long sloping forehead, makes the Eider easy to identify. **Habitat** low rocky and sandy shores and offshore waters; rarely away from the sea. **Nest** in the north on rocks, often amongst low plants, usually in colonies. Lays 4–6 greenish, olive or buff eggs, in a nest thickly lined with down. **Food** largely molluscs and crustacea taken in underwater dives. **Voice** includes musical crooning notes from drakes.

Common Scoter

Melanitta nigra

Length: 47 cm

Weight: 700–1300 g

4

W

Distant flocks of dark birds bobbing on the sea like corks, or flying low over the waves in long straggling lines, will often prove to be Common Scoters. They are busy, buoyant diving birds, happy in the roughest sea. When seen closely they reveal an elegant form, with a shapely head on a thin neck, and quite a long, pointed tail. Drakes are black all over except for a yellow patch on the bill. Females are dark brown, with the lower half of the face pale. **Habitat** the sea, often miles offshore over sandy shoals, or closer in in wide sandy bays. Small parties regularly occur inland in summer and autumn, staying for a short time on a reservoir before moving on. **Nest** in heather close to water in northern moors, or near large Irish loughs; but in the British Isles a rare nesting bird. **Food** mostly molluscs, taken underwater—feeding flocks may be very large. Dives rarely exceed half a minute, as it prefers moderate depths even if far offshore. **Voice** includes a harsh growl from the duck and musical whistling and piping notes from drakes.

Goldeneye
Bucephala clangula

Length: 45 cm
4

Weight: 500–1200 g
W

This is a much scarcer diving duck than either the Tufted or the Pochard, and although not rare it is never familiar to non-birdwatchers. Compared with most ducks it is very active and lively, often in rapid flight with whistling wings. It is shy and easily disturbed. Drakes are dazzling white with black on the back and head; in front of the yellow eye is a large white spot. Ducks are duller, grey with white wing patches, a white collar (absent on juveniles) and a dark brown head. Ducks and immatures tend to look rather small, round-backed, large-headed and very dark. Large groups may be almost overlooked as most will be underwater at any one moment. **Habitat** sheltered coastal waters, large lakes and reservoirs, flooded pits, even small pools high up on moors in winter. **Nest** in holes in trees, but most of our very few pairs use special nest-boxes in Scotland. **Food** almost entirely animal, especially molluscs and crustacea, eaten underwater. An expert diver. **Voice** not often heard, but ducks have a deep growl, especially as they take flight, and displaying drakes make a strange rasping, metallic sound. Wings whistle loudly in flight.

Red-breasted Merganser

Merganser serrator

Length: 58 cm

Weight: 850–1300 g

4   **R**

Though as long as a Mallard, the Merganser is much more slender; it swims low in the water, and is an expert diver. The drake in full plumage is a beautiful bird, with glossy green head, white neck, rufous breast and grey, black and white body and wings. In summer it becomes more like the duck, with a brownish-grey body and a ginger-brown head, blending into a white chin and foreneck. All have a wispy crest and a long, slender red bill; the drake also has vivid red eyes. In flight they are long, slim and fast-flying, showing much white on the wing. **Habitat** lakes, rivers and sheltered coastal waters. **Nest** on the ground amongst long vegetation close to water, or in a shallow burrow. The duck lays 7–12 dull buff eggs, and incubates them for 29 days; only she tends the young. **Food** fish, caught and securely held by the toothed edges of the hooked bill. **Voice** insignificant—a harsh growl from the duck, especially on taking flight, and whistling noises from the displaying male.

Goosander
Mergus merganser

Length: 65 cm

Weight: 1·25–1·9 kg

5

R

Resplendent in green-glossed black, white, grey and rich pink, a drake Goosander is extremely handsome. He lacks the red eyes of the Merganser, but the long bill is deep red. Ducks are much more like Mergansers but may be distinguished by the cleaner blue-grey of the body, the dark-brown, less ginger, head and the sharply-defined white throat with a band of brown beneath. All Goosanders show much white in flight and look very long and streamlined. **Habitat** chiefly freshwaters, including broad rivers in the breeding season; large lakes and reservoirs in winter. **Nest** near a river or lake in the north and west of Britain, usually in a cavity in a tree but also amongst boulders and in boxes. Lays 7–13 eggs, creamy white and unmarked; the duck incubates for 34–35 days. The ducklings leave the nest after 2–3 days and are tended by the duck alone. **Food** almost entirely fish, caught by diving expertly. Like the Merganser, the Goosander grasps fish in its serrated bill. **Voice** infrequently heard—a low growling note from the female.

Ruddy Duck

Oxyura jamaicensis

Length: 36–43 cm

Weight: 350–750 g

4

R

Introduced into southern England and now well established, especially in the midlands, this species originates from America but has found our lakes and reservoirs just to its liking.　No other species has its round, dumpy shape, with a stiff, pointed tail, short wings and large bill. Drakes are rufous-brown with a black cap and pure white face, contrasting with a bright blue bill.　In winter they are duller but still white-faced; and their tail still distinguishes them.　Ducks are always dull brown, with a pale face crossed by a dark band. Ruddy Ducks dive expertly, but fly less well than most ducks. **Habitat** fresh water with a dense growth of reeds or similar plants at the edge, although more open waters are used in winter. **Nest** amongst reeds and rushes; it makes a large nest of leaves and stems, well-hidden.　**Food** mostly insect larvae, seeds and similar small items sieved from mud on the lake bottom.　**Voice** rarely calls.

Marsh Harrier
Circus aeruginosus

Length: 50 cm   Weight: 320–650 g (male)

4   550–1250 g (female)   **R/W**

This rare bird is always an exciting find, whether over its few nesting haunts or at some marsh or reedy swamp on migration. Females and immature males (illustrated) are bulky, broad-winged harriers, with dark brown plumage, except for a cream top to the head and paler shoulders. Males in fully developed adult plumage are far less frequent. They then show pale heads, bright buff patches on the inner wing, black wing-tips and pale grey areas in the wing and tail. This patchy, striking effect is very distinctive. The male is more lightly built than the female, but both have a low, slow flight, with a few wingbeats between glides that are made with slightly raised wings. They may sometimes soar very high, looking much more like Buzzards, but longer-tailed. **Habitat** extensive reed-beds and other marshy ground. **Nest** amongst reeds, mostly in East Anglia. Lays 4–5 whitish eggs, which are incubated for 30–38 days; until the young have left the nest the male hunts for the female and passes food to her in the air. The young move out of the nest after 35–40 days but are not fledged for another 21 days. **Food** largely small mammals and small birds; also frogs, eggs and other items taken from the ground. **Voice** rarely heard outside the breeding season.

Hen Harrier

Circus cyaneus

Length: 48 cm

Weight: 300–700 g

4

R

This is the most common harrier. The adult males are very different from the females. They are more lightly built and mostly pale grey, paler beneath and with a white rump patch, black wing-tips and a dark trailing edge to each wing. Females and young birds are much less conspicuous, being dark brown above and rich buff below. They have barred tails and a prominent patch of white on the rump, absent on the Marsh Harrier and the Buzzard. They have a flight action similar to that of the Marsh Harrier, but it is more buoyant. **Habitat** largely upland moors, conifer plantations and boggy areas in Wales, northern England, Ireland, Scotland and the Orkney Islands; more widespread in winter, visiting coastal marshes and open pasture-land. **Nest** in long heather and rushes, or amongst young conifers. It makes a flat pad of heather stems on which 4–5 bluish-white eggs are laid in May. Incubation is by the female, for 29–30 days; the male hunts and passes food to the female as she leaves the nest. The young fly after 5–6 weeks. **Food** small mammals and birds caught by surprise on or near the ground, after low hunting flight with wings raised in a shallow V during glides. **Voice** near the nest, a rapid chatter, less regular from the female—*chik-ik-ik-ik-ik*.

Sparrowhawk
Accipiter nisus

Length: 27–37 cm
4

Weight: 100–200 g (male)
185–345 g (female)
R

A widespread recovery from a serious decline in the 1960s has made Sparrowhawks again quite frequent, except in eastern England; but they are much more secretive than either Kestrel or Buzzard. A fast disappearing shadow sweeping between trees or dashing over a hedge is all that is likely to be seen of these broad-winged, long-tailed hawks, except when they are displaying over their nesting woods in spring. Their blunt wing-tips and flight action—a series of rapid flaps between flat glides—distinguish them from the Kestrel, but only a close view shows that they have bars (instead of the Kestrel's streaks) on the breast. Males are small and lightly built, bluish above and orange beneath. The much bigger females (illustrated) are browner and greyer. **Habitat** woodland of all sorts, and adjacent farmland; more open ground in winter, even marshes and moors. **Nest** a flat platform of sticks close to the main stem of a tree, preferably a conifer. Incubates 4–5 whitish eggs, blotched with red-brown, for 32–35 days. **Food** almost entirely small birds. As with most predators, the number of Sparrowhawks is determined by the number of small birds available; the hawks have no long term effect on the population of their prey. **Voice** a rapid, screaming *kek-kek-kek*.

Buzzard
Buteo buteo

Length: 55 cm
5

Weight: 450–1350 g
R

With the exception of the Golden Eagle, this is the most majestic bird of prey in Britain. In Wales and southwest England it may also be the most common. The shallow V of the wings during its soaring, circling flight is a helpful feature for identification, combined with the breadth and considerable span of its wings—it is *much* larger than a crow. Though variable in pattern, most Buzzards are brown above and creamy below, with heavy brown spots across the breast, and dark barring on the wings. **Habitat** mixed farmland and woods, usually in hilly districts, but it is not a mountain bird. Often high on barren moors when hunting. **Nest** in a tree, rarely on a cliff ledge, but frequently in an inaccessible bush growing from a crag. Lays 2–3 eggs in a bulky, flat-topped nest of sticks and stems, often decorated with fresh sprays of greenery. Incubation lasts 34–38 days and the young fly after 6–7 weeks. **Food** chiefly small mammals up to rabbit size, but also carrion, worms, beetles and some birds—it is a species harmless to farmers' stock. It spots its food from the air or while perching on a wall, fence or telegraph pole—a big bird of prey on a roadside pole will be a Buzzard, not an eagle! **Voice** includes mewing notes and a powerful, far-carrying scream, *peeyah*.

Golden Eagle

Aquila chrysaetos

Length: 80 cm

Weight: 2·85–6·5 kg

6

R

Majestic in its appearance and powers of flight, the Golden Eagle is certainly one of Britain's most important birds. Its population is thriving here, in comparison with declines elsewhere in its wide range. Nevertheless, an encounter with a Golden Eagle is a moment of rare and tremendous excitement. It spends hours each day sitting still, hard to see; but once in action it is supremely impressive. Its flying abilities—both its effortless soaring and, more breathtaking, its high speed manoeuvres—are certainly remarkable. At a height its size (with a wing-span often over 2 m) is not always obvious, but its stability, longish neck, long broad tail and wings longer than those of a Buzzard help to identify it. Young birds (illustrated) have white on the wings and tail and are very distinct, but adults are brown all over, with paler bands across the upper wings, and a pale nape. **Habitat** mostly remote uplands in Scotland, with a pair or two in England. More rarely forested areas and sea cliffs. **Nest** on a cliff ledge, in a large tree or even on sloping lower ground in some places. Two eggs, marked with red-brown, are laid in April and incubated for six weeks. Frequently only one chick survives to fly after 11 weeks. **Food** largely hares, Red Grouse and Ptarmigan. Also takes dead lambs, deer calves and other carrion. **Voice** a variety of yelps.

Osprey
Pandion haliaetus

Length: 50–57 cm
5

Weight: 1–2 kg
S

Bigger and longer-winged than a Buzzard, but less magnificent, perhaps, than a Golden Eagle, the Osprey is a glorious bird. Made famous by its much-publicized return to nest in Scotland after extermination from Britain by man, the Osprey is still an exciting spectacle and a rare find away from its few public nesting sites. In flight it shows large areas of white beneath, with no hint of buff or brown except on a faint breast-band; so its gleaming appearance is quite unlike that of even a pale Buzzard. Under the wings are black bars and spots; the whole upperside is dark brown except for a paler tail and a whitish crown. A black band through the eye finishes off its unique appearance. It has long wings, usually angled slightly at the carpal joint, which is raised in front view giving a slightly bowed look. **Habitat** near water—lakes, rivers or quiet coastal districts. **Nest** on rocky islets and in tall pines. Lays 2–3 eggs, richly blotched with red-brown, which are incubated for five weeks in a huge stick nest. Young fly after $7\frac{1}{2}$ weeks or more; they are distinguishable by the buff feather edges on their upperside. **Food** almost entirely fish, caught in a spectacular, often twisting, plunge-dive ending in a loud splash. **Voice** near the nest is a shrill, quite musical whistle, rapidly repeated: *chew chew chew chew chew.*

Kestrel
Falco tinnunculus

Length: 33 cm
4
Weight: 120–300 g
R

The commonest bird of prey over most of Britain and Ireland, and always the most likely to be seen in the south and east of England, the Kestrel is a familiar bird of rural areas and suburbia. Some even penetrate our largest cities. Its most distinctive feature by far is its frequent habit of hovering, hanging as if on a string, its wings beating rapidly or flickering lightly according to changes in the wind. With outspread tail and head bent forward to view the ground below, the shape of the hunting Kestrel is instantly recognizable. Many people mistakenly call it a Sparrowhawk (a bird which does *not* hover) but the Kestrel is the roadside vole-hunter which drops into the grass at the slightest sign of a meal. Kestrels have long, slender wings, and a slender tail. The pale rufous upper parts (with grey head and tail on the male), dark tail-band and blackish-brown wing-tips are good distinguishing features. **Habitat** open ground, from high moorland to coastal marshes and dunes; farmland and parks, urban areas. **Nest** on a sheltered ledge of a cliff, in an old Crow's nest, cavities in trees, barns or other buildings. Lays 4–5 eggs from April onwards, and incubates them for 27–29 days; the young fly after 27–30 days. **Food** largely mice and voles, but many beetles and worms are taken; also small birds. **Voice** a shrill *kee-kee-kee-keee*.

Merlin

Falco columbarius

Length: 27–32 cm

4

Weight: 125–230 g
(male)
155–300 g (female)

R

The little, spirited Merlin is a rare and declining bird of the upland moors. In build it is more like a small Peregrine than the longer-tailed, blunter-winged Kestrel. Its behaviour, however, is all its own, its dashing, low-level flight with rapid wingbeats (but few glides) being especially characteristic. The observer may have to settle for no more than that, as it speeds off out of sight, leaving little chance for much plumage detail to be seen. Females (illustrated) are dark, earthy brown without the rufous of a Kestrel, and have a cream-barred tail. The smaller, lightweight males are blue-grey above, orange-buff below, with vivid yellow feet. **Habitat** breeds in moorland heather, on coastal dunes, or in scattered hillside scrub. In winter it visits coastal marshes and farmland where there are finch flocks. **Nest** on the ground or in a tree, on a pad of heather stems or in an old Crow's nest. Lays four eggs in May. Incubation lasts 28–32 days and the young fly after almost 28 days. **Food** small birds, taken in the air or from the ground, even including nestlings, but usually pipits or similar species caught after a fast, aerobatic chase. Also moths and other insects. **Voice** near the nest, usually a rapid chatter, *quik-ikikikikik*, or a deeper *quek-ek-ek-ek* from the female.

Hobby
Falco subbuteo

Length: 32 cm
4

Weight: 130–230 g
(male)
140–340 g (female)
S

Of all the speedy, long-winged falcons this is the most agile and graceful in action. Its appearance always brings a thrill of excitement and admiration as it soars and glides or races through the air with deep, fast beats of its long, swept-back, pointed wings. The most obvious feature at reasonable range is a white patch on the sides of the neck, contrasting with a black moustache. At a distance little else may be made out except a generally dark appearance with little contrast. Close views reveal broad black streaking on a pale underside, a dark grey back and tail and some rufous on the thighs and under the tail if the bird is adult. But for identification the bird's slim, short-tailed shape is more useful than its plumage features. **Habitat** mixed trees and open ground, either heaths with pines and forest edges or farmland with scattered copses. **Nest** in an old Crow's or Rook's nest in a tall tree, often a pine, in southern and central England. Lays three pale, blotchy brown eggs, which are incubated for 28 days; the young fly after 28–32 days, leaving the nest in early August. **Food** small birds and insects caught (and often eaten) in the air. **Voice** a variable, but often shrill, clear *kew-kew-kew-kew-kew*.

Peregrine
Falco peregrinus

Length: 37–48 cm
4

Weight: 580–750 g
(male)
925–1300 g (female)
R

Although only an inch or two longer than the biggest Hobby, the smallest male Peregrine is nearly twice as heavy; females are about five times the weight of an average Kestrel. These facts give an idea of how much heavier and stronger a Peregrine is in comparison with its smaller cousins. It is broad in almost every proportion, yet appears graceful and buoyant in the air, with smoothly swept-back wings which make a bird overhead look anchor-shaped. In direct flight it alternates deep and quick wingbeats (not unlike those of a pigeon) with flat glides. It can accelerate impressively, and may turn down into a near-vertical stoop onto its prey. It is also capable of the most exciting aerobatics around its nesting cliff. Adults are blue-grey above and paler below, barred with grey and often tinged with buff or pink with a whiter chest. Young birds are browner and streaked. All have a broad black moustache or facial patch and a whiter neck. **Habitat** almost anywhere, but breeds in hilly, moorland and coastal districts; in winter it is often on marshes. **Nest** on a cliff ledge. Lays 3–4 blotched brown eggs in April, incubating for 28–29 days. The young fly when 5–6 weeks old. **Food** chiefly birds, especially pigeons, usually taken in the air, often in level flight. **Voice** a variety of rapid, chattering notes which can develop into a hoarse, outraged scream, *kek-kek-kek-kek-kek, kwaah-kwaah-kwaah-kwairk-kwairk.*

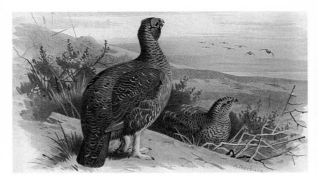

Red Grouse

Lagopus lagopus

Length: 38 cm

Weight: 600–700 g

4

R

A challenging cock grouse, standing atop a tuft of heather, or flying up in a display flight above the moor, is a fine sight, typical of the broad, rolling heather-covered moorlands of northern Britain and Ireland. Its habitat is in decline, especially in Wales, being changed into pasture for sheep, or planted up with conifers. The Red Grouse remains numerous only where the moor is managed for it, to give plenty of birds to shoot. A close view reveals a remarkably beautiful bird, richly patterned with red-brown, blackish and buff. In flight it is Partridge-like, but darker and with a blackish tail; it dashes away with whirring wings, and then will glide with its wings bowed stiffly down. **Habitat** principally heather moor, but also found in lesser numbers on boggy ground with rushes and heather admixed. **Nest** on the ground in heather or rushes. Lays 6–11 eggs, rich buff-brown, heavily and intricately patterned darker. Incubation lasts 21–26 days and is carried out solely by the female. The young fly when still quite small, after 12–13 days. **Food** largely shoots, flowers and seeds of heather; chicks feed on insects. **Voice** very distinctive and far-carrying—a cackling, staccato *kowk, kok-ok-ok-ok-ok, kowk, k-krrrrk-kok, gobak bak-bak-bak.*

Red-legged Partridge

Alectoris rufa

Length: 34 cm

Weight: 400–540 g

4

R

This large partridge, an introduced species, is common in open farmland over much of eastern and midland England. Small parties may be seen moving slowly over fields, crouched like mounds of brown earth and shuffling forward until disturbed, when they stretch their legs and run off at high speed. If they fly, they show a rufous tail and are hard to tell from Grey Partridges. On the ground it is easier to see the white face, surrounded by black, the red bill and red legs. The flanks are more boldly striped with black, white and red-brown. The upper parts are uniform brown without the streaks of the Grey Partridge. **Habitat** mainly sandy heaths, chalky ground, open fields and dunes. **Nest** on the ground; lays 10–16 brown and buff mottled eggs in April or May. Incubation lasts 23–24 days. The female may lay two clutches in separate nests; the male incubates one clutch and tends the young when they have hatched. **Food** mainly vegetable matter. **Voice** is distinctive. Gives a sharp *uk-uk* when flushed. Other calls include *chuk chuk chukar*, *chuka chuka* and harsh, hissing variants. Often calls from an elevated perch—a pile of straw bales or even the top of a barn.

Grey Partridge

Perdix perdix

Length: 30 cm

Weight: 320–430 g

4

R

This, our native partridge, is more widely distributed than the larger Red-legged Partridge, an introduced bird, and is commoner in the north and west. It also occurs in Ireland. It is a rather less noticeable bird, keeping more carefully to cover as a rule. Unlike the Red-legged Partridge it has no white on the face, which is a soft shade of orange-brown; it has a grey breast and belly, all closely and finely barred, chestnut barring on the flanks and a curved patch of dark brown in the centre of the under parts. It is streaked with buff on the back and sides, presenting overall a colour mixture subtler than that of its relative. In flight it alternates rapid wingbeats with short glides on stiffly bowed wings, and shows a chestnut tail. **Habitat** agricultural country, heaths, dunes; requires more cover than the Red-leg. **Nest** on the ground in the bottom of a hedge or bush. The 9–20 eggs are plain olive-buff, laid in April or May and incubated by the female for 23–25 days. The young birds fly when still only half-grown. **Food** largely vegetable, but also ants, worms, slugs. Insects are important for the chicks. **Voice** a hoarse, slightly rasping, rhythmic *kierric* or *ker-wit*, with a distinctive, pleasing, creaky effect. A quick *kit kit* when flushed.

Pheasant

Phasianus colchicus

Length: 53–63 cm (female)
75–90 cm (male)
5

Weight: 750–1800 g
R

Few birds are quite so readily recognized as the Pheasant. Familiar to all, the cock, especially, is hard to mistake—a splendid bird with a slow, regal walk, raised head and long, pointed tail. If the bird is disturbed, its walk can quickly change into a rapid , crouching run, or a sudden burst of noisy, whirring flight. The beautiful green head, often with a white collar, bold bars of purple-black on its rufous and coppery breast, dark, and largely rusty-brown upper parts and black-barred tail, belong only to the male. The hen is much more quietly clothed in sober pale brown. Young birds are very much like the female. **Habitat** a variety of countryside with cover in the form of old hedgerows, woods and spinneys, near open ground such as fields and commons. Also reed-beds. **Nest** on the ground in thick cover. It lays 8–15 eggs, pale olive-brown, from May onwards and incubates them for 22–27 days. Very many Pheasants are, of course, artificially reared for shooting. **Food** varied vegetable and animal matter picked from the ground. **Voice** of male is a loud *korrk kok* or *karrk karrk*, often accompanied by a loud threshing of wings. Often very noisy at dusk.

Water Rail

Rallus aquaticus

Length: 28 cm

Weight: 95–160 g

4

R

Although elusive, skulking and more often heard than seen, the Water Rail is not always shy; it may sometimes appear in the open, especially in colder weather. But usually it remains hidden deep in reeds or other swampy vegetation, for movement through which it is perfectly adapted, with a long, slender bill and a remarkably thin body. From the side it looks more solid than it really is. Close views show it to be a very beautiful bird—rich olive-brown with dark streaks above, becoming blue-grey on the throat, foreneck and breast, and barred black-and-white on its sides. Under the short, raised tail is a pale patch. The long bill is vivid red with a black ridge in summer, a duller red in winter and on young birds. **Habitat** any waterside areas where there is ample cover—reed-beds, wet alder thickets, edges of rivers and ditches. **Nest** amongst reeds and rushes, often raised above ground or water level. Lays 6–11 pale eggs, with small dark blotches, in a small, neat nest, from April to July. Incubation lasts 19–20 days and is carried out by both sexes. The young fly after 7–8 weeks. **Food** varied—insects and spiders, molluscs, small fish, roots, berries, seeds—even young birds. **Voice** is a useful clue to its presence: a sharp, repeated *kik-kik-kik*, often at dusk or after dark, and various loud, pig-like squeals.

Moorhen
Gallinula chloropus

Length: 33 cm
4

Weight: 200–380 g
R

The shape and plumage of this bird are equally distinctive. Its small, slender head (often held well forward), deep body and short, cocked tail give it a most unusual silhouette, while the combination of red and yellow bill, green legs with a red garter, and dark plumage with white flank stripes and white under the tail, make it unmistakable. The upperside is a deep, glossy olive-brown, the neck and breast dark slate-grey with a silky sheen. Young birds are duller and much browner, with a greenish bill, but their shape, and nervous lively actions are still characteristic. On the water Moorhens swim with a rhythmic bobbing of the head; on land they flirt and cock the tail, revealing the white patch below, and run quickly into cover if approached. **Habitat** still and slow-flowing water from tiny ponds up to reservoirs, with plentiful vegetation on the banks and open, grassy areas nearby. **Nest** near the water's edge amongst vegetation, even in bushes or quite high in trees. Lays 5–11 buffish eggs with copious markings from April onwards. They hatch after 19–22 days; chicks are blackish with red on the bill. **Food** mainly plant material—seeds, fruits and berries. Also slugs, worms, tadpoles, small fish. **Voice** includes a loud, sudden *curruc* and *kitik*. May be heard in flight at night.

Coot

Fulica atra

Length: 37 cm

Weight: 450–850 g

4

R

Whether on broad stretches of open water, swimming amongst flooded trees and bushes, or grazing on grassy areas beside a lake, the Coot is easy to recognize. It swims with its tail low (not cocked like a Moorhen's); this gives it a round-backed look. It has no white on the flanks or under the tail, and no brown in the plumage at any age. It is wholly slaty grey and black except for a white bill and facial shield. Young birds are greyer, with a white face and throat. Coots dive expertly, often with a forward leap, and bob back up like corks; but they are equally at home on land, when they look big, round, almost tail-less and very large-footed. **Habitat** usually waters larger than ponds, but it requires cover for nesting, if only an overhanging flooded bush. In winter flocks may be found on reservoirs, lakes and flooded pits. **Nest** is amongst reeds or bushes in water; lays 6–9 eggs from late March onwards in a nest which may be quite bulky up above water level. Eggs hatch after 21–24 days; the chicks have red down on the face and neck. **Food** largely green stems, grass and water-weeds obtained by diving or grazing. **Voice** a loud, often abrupt and metallic, *kowk, kewk*; young birds begging for food call noisily, with whistling notes.

Oystercatcher
Haematopus ostralegus

Length: 43 cm

Weight: 450–550 g

4

R

Oystercatchers are a familiar feature of sheltered coasts with grassy strands, shingle beaches and sandy bays in the north and west, their loud calling echoing across the still water on a warm summer evening. They are equally characteristic (in Britain) of northern river valleys far from the sea—but most people, perhaps, think of them as autumn and winter birds on all our sandy and muddy shores and estuaries. In some areas flocks may reach many thousands of birds, congregating in dense packs at high tide. In flight they create a blizzard of black and white; in resting flocks the pied plumage appears slashed with the vivid orange of their bills. **Habitat** coastal regions of all sorts. Also grassy valleys and riverside shingle in the north, but otherwise rather scarce inland. **Nest** on the ground in shingle or on turf; it lays three mottled eggs which hatch after 25–28 days' incubation by both sexes. The young quickly leave the nest and fly after 34–37 days. **Food** chiefly molluscs, crustacea, worms and insects—cockles are favoured, not oysters! Feeding birds disperse evenly over mudflats, in some areas also visiting nearby fields to probe for worms. **Voice** is distinctive, often loud and strident. Clear, shrill *kleep-kleep* and short *kip kip*; from late winter to late summer calls often develop into a long, rapid trill.

Avocet
Recurvirostra avosetta

Length: 42 cm
4
Weight: 250–350 g
R

This rare and extremely local wader is seen by thousands of visitors to the East Anglian reserves where it breeds and on the few estuaries of the southwest where some Avocets spend the winter. Emblem of the Royal Society for the Protection of Birds, it is a symbol of successful conservation, having recolonized Britain after years of absence and become well-established because of protection and habitat management. It is quite unmistakeable (though perhaps easy to overlook on a beach full of white gulls)—a gleaming, satiny white all over, except for curved bands of black over the back and wings, and black wing-tips. It is very long-legged and extremely graceful on the ground, but rather more hurried in the air. The most remarkable feature is the shape of the bill—very slender, pointed and sharply upcurved. **Habitat** lagoons of fresh and brackish water, muddy estuaries with shallow water. **Nest** on the ground in colonies near lagoons. Four eggs are laid in May and hatch after 22–24 days. **Food** largely minute creatures sieved from water by a sideways sweep of the bill as the bird wades slowly forward. **Voice** is distinctive, a musical, clear whistle, *kloot* or *klewt*.

Little Ringed Plover

Charadrius dubius

Length: 15 cm

2

Weight: 30–50 g

S

A little shorter, but much more lightweight and slim in build than the Ringed Plover, this species is more of an inland bird and not often to be seen on the open shore. It can most easily be distinguished in flight, when it shows no white wing-bar, but a good view on the ground will reveal a black bill with just a touch of colour at its base (that of the Ringed Plover is half orange), dull (instead of orange) legs and a bright yellow ring encircling the eye. Any similar bird seen in winter will be the (larger) Ringed Plover, because the Little Ringed is only a summer visitor. On arrival in spring pairs soon settle at a gravel-pit, but may face competition from their larger relatives already established there. Song flights and territorial disputes are frequent. **Habitat** edges of freshwater such as flooded pits and reservoirs, sand and gravel, even waste and derelict industrial ground such as spoil heaps near pools. In England only. **Nest** on the ground; it lays four eggs, usually in May. These hatch after 24–26 days, and the young fly when 24 days old. They lack the black head markings of the adult. **Food** largely insects. **Voice** is a useful character, being quite distinct from that of other plovers—a short, rather low *pew* or *piw*. Display and alarm calls are more prolonged and trilled.

Ringed Plover *Charadrius hiaticula*

Length: 18 cm   Weight: 50–90 g

3   **R**

Small, round-bodied and boldly patterned, the Ringed Plover is one of our commoner waders, but it is often subject to considerable disturbance on the sand and shingle beaches it favours in summer. In winter large numbers arrive on our beaches and estuaries, though their flocks are rarely so large and dense as those of the Dunlin or Knot. Often mixing with other small waders, the Ringed Plovers are identifiable by their short bills and distinctive feeding action. They run a few feet, stop to pick something from the ground, then run a bit more, perhaps pausing to look nervously around before moving on. They have brown backs, white undersides, a broad black breastband and black head stripes. In flight they show a conspicuous white stripe along the wing. **Habitat** sandy and pebbly shores in summer. Nests increasingly beside gravel-pits inland; less often now on sandy heathland. In winter, sandy, muddy and rocky beaches; by all sorts of freshwater inland, on passage. **Nest** on the ground. Four eggs, laid in May or June in a shallow scoop, hatch after 24–25 days; the young fly at 25 days old. **Food** includes molluscs, insects, worms. **Voice** a liquid, fluty *too-i*, the second part higher. The song, given in a display flight with wings fully outstretched, is a complex trilling version of the ordinary calls.

Golden Plover

Pluvialis apricaria

Length: 27 cm

Weight: 150–250 g

4

R

Typically smaller, more lightly built and neater looking than the Grey Plover, this species has a similar plumage pattern but is always much more brown or yellow. In summer British breeding birds have black and yellow speckling above, with the sides of the neck and flanks whitish; there is a variable amount of black on the face and under parts. Winter birds are also spangled yellow and black, but a close view is necessary to see the detail. Normally they look golden-brown. In flight Golden Plovers are round-bodied, but have long, pointed wings. They have a streaky white wing-bar, but a dark rump. Often they feed in fields with Lapwings but in the air separate into faster-flying groups. **Habitat** broad, rolling upland moors; in winter, fields and salt-marshes, less often the muddy shore. **Nest** on the ground in short heather or bilberry, or short grass. Four eggs are incubated for 27–28 days. **Food** insects, worms, seeds, berries. Flocks spread over fields, the birds tipping forward every few feet to pick up food. They may be harried by gulls. **Voice** readily gives away their presence should a few birds be mixed with Lapwings—a musical, liquid whistle, *tlui*. On the moors, a more drawn-out version of this note and a rich, trilling song given in a special display flight.

Grey Plover

Pluvialis squatarola

Length: 28 cm

Weight: 200–300 g

4

W

The handsome summer plumage of the Grey Plover—spangled with black, white and silvery grey above and mostly intensely black beneath—is not often seen by most birdwatchers in the British Isles. The bird is more familiar in autumn and winter, when it looks dull and grey. Autumn juveniles are browner, and likely to be confused with the commoner Golden Plover, but they are bigger, with a larger head, bill and eye. A close view of an adult shows the grey to be made up of complex black-and-white patterning. In flight at all ages the species is always best distinguished by the black armpit-like patches beneath the base of each wing; these show up well, even at long range. The white rump is also unlike the uniformly dark one of the Golden Plover. **Habitat** mostly the seashore; uncommon inland. Does not breed in Britain. **Food** a mixture of small molluscs, worms and crustacea picked from the mud in typical plover manner, the bird tipping forward at intervals between short runs. **Voice** highly distinctive—a longer note than the Golden Plover's, and with three syllables, the middle one lower—*tlee-oo-ee*.

Lapwing

Vanellus vanellus

Length: 30 cm

Weight: 175–290 g

4

R

Lapwings flicker black-and-white as they fly; their broad, rounded wings, glistening white under parts and white rump, combined with the slow, flappy flight, make them hard to mistake. A close view is needed to see the beautifully iridescent green of the upper parts, with a touch of purple and copper at the bend of the wing, the black and buff facial pattern, wispy black crest and deep pink legs. Young birds have less crest, and bright buff feather edges on the back. The Lapwing's stop-and-start feeding action is distinctive even at long range; a short, quick walk followed by a dip of the body to pick from the ground with the short bill. In the spring cock Lapwings display over their territory with a remarkable twisting flight. **Habitat** open spaces with bare soil or short vegetation—farmland, moors, commons and close-cropped salt-marshes. Lapwings often congregate on muddy edges of lakes and reservoirs in late summer and autumn. **Nest** on the ground in a field or on moorland edge. Lays four mottled eggs which hatch after 24–27 days. **Food** mostly insects, also worms, spiders, seeds. **Voice** a nasal, wheezy *peer-wit, weep-wit*, etc; in display a prolonged *peerrweet-weet-weet* and a loud wing noise.

71

Knot

Calidris canutus

Length: 25 cm

Weight: 150 g

3

W/M

The Knot is often called a 'middle sized' wader, being bigger and stockier than birds such as the Dunlin but markedly smaller and shorter-legged than the Redshank or the Godwits. It is a rather nondescript bird (illustrated) in winter, looking rather pale greyish all over, paler below than above, but with little contrast. It may therefore, as often as not, be picked out by a process of elimination, because it lacks the distinguishing features of anything else! It is pale, almost whitish, on the rump and has a thin white wing-bar; the bill is rather short and dark, the legs short and greenish. It is a splendid bird in breeding plumage, however, being spangled black and buff above, with rich chestnut red all over the head, neck and under parts. **Habitat** muddy estuaries, often far out on huge mudflats; total numbers often run into thousands. Smaller numbers in more restricted bays, and occasionally inland on passage. **Food** includes molluscs and crustacea picked from the mud. Flocks feed in a distinctive fashion, advancing over the mud in dense crowds. **Voice** little heard except as a low, indistinct chatter from flocks; also an occasional liquid *quick-ik* in flight.

Sanderling

Calidris alba

Length: 20 cm

3

Weight: 50–70 g

W/M

A small wader which may be confused with the Dunlin,
the Sanderling is a more active bird with a rapid run on
twinkling black legs, and with a shorter, straight, black
bill.   In spring adults develop a richly mottled plumage
of chestnut and black (often rather pale on the breast) with
clean white under parts—they never have any suggestion
of streaking below the breastband.   In autumn some
retain reddish on the neck, and juveniles are buff on the
neck and boldly spangled with black above.   Otherwise
they, and winter adults, are the palest of the small waders,
gleaming white below and silvery-grey above.   The dark
wing coverts may show as a spot at the bend of the wing
at rest; in flight the wing has a broader and more striking
white stripe than that of a Dunlin.   The rump is similar
to the Dunlin's, dark with white sides.   Sanderlings like
to feed close to the edge of breaking waves on a clean
sandy beach, running in and out to pick food from the
disturbed sand.   They more rarely probe about in muddy
flats like Dunlins, and even then their quicker action is
noticeable.   **Habitat** sandy and muddy shores; infrequent inland, where most often seen for short spells in
May.   **Food** sandhoppers and other crustacea, molluscs.
Voice quite distinct from that of Dunlin—a short, sharp
twik, twik.

Little stint

Calidris minuta

Length: 13 cm

Weight: 25–30 g

2

M

This tiny wader is barely larger than a sparrow, but its longer legs and bill give it such different proportions than its size may not be immediately apparent without direct comparison. Seen with a Dunlin, it does look smaller and more delicate, with a shorter, straighter bill. Stints are also quicker and more nervous in their actions. The clean white under parts catch the eye. Most birds seen in Britain are juveniles in autumn, and these look warm, rufous-brown above, marked with black and cream, with a pale V shape on the back. The breast is creamy-buff, streaked only on the sides. The legs look black. **Habitat** muddy edges of freshwater, less often muddy seashores. Most frequent in the east of Britain, but not uncommon by reservoirs inland in some years. Little Stints occur with Dunlins as a rule, sometimes accompanied by Curlew Sandpipers. They are scarce in spring and rare in winter or summer. **Food** tiny crustacea, worms and insects, picked from the surface of mud. **Voice** an abrupt, sharp *tic* or *tit*, sometimes developing into a stutter as the bird takes flight—*ti-ti-tit tit*.

Curlew Sandpiper
Calidris ferruginea

Length: 19 cm
Weight: 50–60 g

3
M

This is a scarce autumn migrant, to be looked for amongst flocks of Dunlins in August and September, although a few do occur in the spring. Compared with a Dunlin it is a little more elegant and refined, with longer legs and a longer, slender, slightly down-curved bill. Adults in summer are beautifully red below and on the head, with a white eye-ring and mottled back; in autumn some birds with the remains of this colour in irregular blotches can be seen. Young birds are like young Dunlins, but less streaked above, having more delicate scaly edgings to the feathers; they are whiter beneath, without the dark flank spots, and are much cleaner, brighter orange-buff or peachy coloured across the breast. The differences become more noticeable if the birds take flight, because they show a broad patch of white across the rump instead of a Dunlin's black central stripe. With their longer legs and more upright stance, Curlew Sandpipers tend to wade more deeply than Dunlins. **Habitat** edges of gravel-pits and reservoirs, shallow lagoons and coastal areas, mostly in the east and south; often with Dunlins and Little Stints. **Food** as for Dunlin. **Voice** may catch the attention in a mixed group: a soft, low *chirrip*, the *r* more or less rolled.

Purple Sandpiper
Calidris maritima

Length: 21 cm
3

Weight: 55–85 g
W

This is a round, dark, confiding bird, larger and heavier in build than a Dunlin, and found not on muddy and sandy beaches, but on the rocky, seaweed- and barnacle-covered shores of Ireland and north and west Britain, with the biggest numbers perhaps in northeast England. It often mixes with Turnstones, whose infectious irritability makes the whole flock less approachable; but on their own Purple Sandpipers will often allow an observer within a few feet. At close range they show a complex pattern of white feather edges on blackish upper parts, a liver-brown neck and head, softly streaked and marked with white around the eye and chin, and white under parts broadly smudged and streaked with grey-brown. The slightly down-curved bill has a patch of yellow or orange at the base; the legs are dull orange or deep yellow. The birds feed at the very edge of the breaking waves, often leaping from rock to rock with open wings, to show a long white wing-stripe and white sides to the rump, which has a particularly broad and black centre. **Habitat** rocky shores. Also about piers and groynes or small stony patches in otherwise sandy beaches. **Food** picked from the weedy tangle, includes molluscs, crustacea, small fish. **Voice** includes thin, high notes usually uttered in flight— *weet, peet-it.*

Dunlin
Calidris alpina

Length: 18 cm

Weight: 40–55 g

3

R

Of all the small waders, the Dunlin is the most widespread; its features should be thoroughly learned, as it forms a useful comparison when identifying something less usual. Dunlins look rather round-shouldered, moving in short runs or in leisurely, plodding style as they pick food from the mud.   Adults in summer have chestnut upper parts, with dark and light streaking; their heads and breasts are paler and greyer, softly streaked, and on the under parts is a large, rather square patch of inky black, not shown by any other small wader.   In winter they are dull, palish grey-brown above, and white below except for a streaky breast.   Young birds in autumn are similar, but much more marked with dark streaks and yellow-buff edges above, and with dark grey spots and mottles along their flanks.   In flight all show a white wing-stripe and a dark rump with prominent white sides.   **Habitat** mudflats and sandy estuaries, smaller bays, less often rocky shores; gravel-pits and reservoirs, salt-marshes and wet fields inland.   Mostly autumn to spring but a few breed on upland moors or coastal marshes in the north and west. **Nest** on the ground.   Four eggs are laid from May onwards.   Both sexes incubate, for a total of 22 days. **Food** largely insects, worms, tiny molluscs and crustacea. **Voice** in flight, is a nasal, short, buzzing *treep* or *dzee*.

Ruff

Philomachus pugnax

Length: 22–30 cm

4

Weight: 100–250 g
(males larger than females) **R**

Ruffs are scarce and irregular as breeding birds, but males
do occur in spring in their fantastic plumage with ear tufts
and enormous neck ruffs of many and varied colours.
Females are brownish, heavily blotched with black. In
winter both are pale grey-brown, often very pale on the
head. Autumn juveniles, perhaps the most familiar of all
Ruffs, are rich buff, hardly marked below, with beautiful
black and buff scaly patterning above. Ruffs are
confusing birds, however, being very variable in size and
colour, with legs of orange, red, green or olive! They are
medium-sized, paler (juveniles more richly patterned)
than Redshanks, with short, slightly curved bills. In
flight they are long- and broad-winged, which gives them
a rather slow, steady action unusual among waders. A
thin white wing-stripe shows well, and the rump has a
pattern more like that of the smaller waders, with a dark
centre and white sides. Ruffs tend to occur in ones and
twos or small parties (larger groups in the few places
where they winter), and are less lively, and far less noisy,
then most other waders. **Habitat** wet fields and mainly
freshwater edges. **Nest** on the ground, very well hidden
in long grass. **Food** largely insects and worms. **Voice**
rarely heard—just a low, quiet *t-wit*.

Snipe

Gallinago gallinago

Length: 26 cm

Weight: 100–150 g

3

R

The bill accounts for nearly one quarter of the Snipe's length. It suits it ideally for probing in soft, oozy mud in marshes and waterside areas, but leaves it in real trouble should it be faced with icy weather. The Snipe is usually seen taking flight in a sudden, zigzag dash, or flying high around a marsh, long bill pointing downwards and wings looking pointed but rather short, flickering rapidly. A close view of one on the ground is a delight—the plumage is a beautiful mixture of browns, buff, black and white, with lengthwise stripes of buff on the back and a striped head. In flight the dark wings show a pale trailing edge. **Habitat** usually wet meadows, beside rivers, lakes and reservoirs or in boggy places; more rarely beside the sea. **Nests** on the ground near damp areas, often in a tussock and well hidden. Incubates four eggs for 20 days; the young fly before they are fully grown. **Food** largely worms, but other items are picked from the mud. The tip of the bill is sensitive and flexible, allowing worms to be found and grasped deep in the mud. **Voice** typically a harsh, grating *scaap* as the bird takes flight. In spring it also gives a lively, rhythmic *chip-per chip-per chip-per*, sometimes from a prominent perch; it also produces the well-known 'drumming', a throbbing hum from its stiffly outspread tail feathers during switchback display flights.

Woodcock

Scolopax rusticola

Length: 34 cm

Weight: 250–350 g

4

R

The Woodcock is usually seen only if put up from cover deep within a wood, or when displaying at dusk in the summer. Woodcocks feed in the evening; during the daytime they tend to be inactive and hidden away, except in hard weather. The general appearance is like that of a large and heavily built Snipe, with a stouter bill and dark bars across the head (instead of lengthwise stripes). A Woodcock also lacks the Snipe's back stripes, but its plumage is a beautifully intricate patterning of browns, buffs and greys. The very large eye is very striking on a bird seen on the ground. The flight of a Woodcock, fast and direct if flushed, is usually more leisurely; in the air it looks much stouter than a Snipe and the wings are broad, though still pointed. **Habitat** damp woods with open, boggy or heathy glades; swampy coverts, ditches and boggy ground with scattered bushes. **Nest** on the ground, not always well hidden, but both the sitting bird and the eggs are well camouflaged. Four eggs, laid in March or April, are incubated by the female for about 20 days. Two broods. **Food** largely worms. **Voice** usually a thin, sharp whistle. This note is interspersed with deep, gruff croaks in the special evening 'roding' flights from March to July—a high-pitched *tsiwick* and *crr crr crr*.

Black-tailed Godwit

Limosa limosa

Length: 40 cm

Weight: 200–400 g

4

R

This is one of the most elegant of all the waders, with both bill and legs extra long in proportion to its body. It also has a spectacular appearance in flight and a richly-patterned breeding plumage, making it one of our most attractive birds. On the ground it is easily confused with a Bar-tailed Godwit, but it has an even longer bill and legs, and in summer its colouring is less uniform. The black bars on the flanks and the white vent differentiate it, and the red areas of the neck and breast are generally paler and more coppery. As soon as it takes flight, at any time of year, any doubt as to its identity is instantly resolved as its broad white rump patch and long, wide white wing-bars contrast vividly with the rest of the plumage, almost as on an Oystercatcher. **Habitat** a few birds breed in Britain in the very few remaining areas of wet meadows and sedge. Otherwise in autumn and winter it occurs on salt-marsh, coastal fields and muddy estuaries. **Nest** on the ground in tall grass; four eggs are laid in May. **Food** chiefly worms, grubs and insects. **Voice** not very often heard, is loud, rather nasal and rapid—*wicka wicka wicka*.

Bar-tailed Godwit

Limosa lapponica

Length: 37 cm

Weight: 250–350 g

4

W/M

Although it does not breed here, the Bar-tailed is in general much commoner than the Black-tailed Godwit. Large flocks over-winter, often mixing with Curlews, Redshanks and Knots. Then they look large and pale, but markedly smaller than the Curlews. Instead of the down-curved bills of the latter, they have beaks which are almost straight, or, if anything, curved a little upwards. The bill also has a bright pinkish base. Winter birds are buff and grey-brown, whiter beneath and with a white rump, but in flight they show no strong wing pattern. Breeding plumage may be seen in the spring, or even late winter, and the males may show a gorgeous deep chestnut red. This colouring extends right beneath the tail, unlike that of the Black-tailed Godwit. The Bar-tailed is also shorter-legged. **Habitat** muddy and sandy coasts, especially the larger estuaries and bays, and coastal fields. **Food** mostly worms, small molluscs and the like. Feeding flocks spread over the mud and have a slow, regular walk, probing deeply as they go. **Voice** rather nasal, a low *kurruk*. This may be more frequently and loudly uttered from flocks on passage.

Whimbrel

Numenius phaeopus

Length: 38 cm

Weight: 350–750 g

4

In appearance very much like a smaller version of the Curlew, the Whimbrel is a much rarer bird, occurring in spring and autumn in southern Britain and breeding in very small numbers in the northern isles. The general appearance is like that of the Curlew, but the bill is distinctly more bent, or angled (rather than smoothly curved), and the plumage rather darker (this is most noticeable in flight). A good view is needed to see the most critical point: the head has a pale line above the eye and a very dark crown with a thin pale central line. **Habitat** coastal areas and inland waters (although it is often recorded simply flying over without stopping). Breeding birds prefer bleak northern moorlands, with heather, cotton grass and broken peat bogs. **Nest** on the ground in dry areas; four eggs are laid in late May or June. Incubation is for 24 days; the chicks soon leave the nest area and fly after about four weeks. **Food** largely worms and insects. **Voice** is one of the best features for identifying this bird and serves to draw attention to parties flying overhead or along the shore—a rapid, even trill, *titititititit.*

Curlew
Numenius arquata

Length: 55 cm

Weight: 600–900 g

4

R

Seen across a mudflat on a dull day, Curlews look large and dull, identifiable only by their characteristic shape, with medium-length legs and long, down-curved bill. Better views reveal an attractive wader in brown and white, with an overall streaked effect, paler beneath. Roosting flocks may number hundreds, but outside the breeding season feeding birds are more dispersed.   On the moors in spring Curlews form a prominent part of the scene, especially as they perform their beautiful song flights over their territories.   In flight they look rather gull-like, but show white extending up the back and are longer both front and rear.   **Habitat** moorland and upland pastures, and also riverside meadows in the breeding season.   Otherwise muddy seashores and salt-marshes; also rocky coasts and low-lying pastures.   **Nest** on the ground.   Four greenish eggs, laid in April or May, are incubated for 28–30 days.   **Food** insects and grubs of all sorts; worms, molluscs and crustacea.   **Voice** usually a liquid, loud *quoi quoi* and *crooee crooee*, sometimes harsher and uttered in rapid succession if alarmed.   Song begins with long, sweet notes which increase in speed; ends in a magnificent bubbling trill.

Spotted Redshank

Tringa erythropus

Length: 30 cm

Weight: 100–200 g

4

M

As it does not breed here, we rarely see the beautiful summer plumage of this wader, except at a few coastal localities where summering flocks occur. Even then, most are in less than perfect trim, so to see a deep black bird, with paler speckling above, is something of an event. Mostly we see autumn juveniles, which are grey-brown above and barred with brown below, and winter adults which are much paler and greyer and largely white below. Juveniles are, therefore, more like Redshanks, but adults are more likely to be taken for the paler Greenshank. All Spotted Redshanks can be distinguished by their straight, thin bill with red at the base, very long red legs and in flight by a white patch on the back, but no wing-bar. On the ground a dark stripe from eye to bill, above which is a striking band of white, gives a distinctive expression to all. **Habitat** muddy creeks and flats and freshwater margins, shallow lagoons. **Food** mainly insects, worms, small fish. Wades deeply and more often swims and upends than other waders, often chasing small fry with rapid and erratic actions. **Voice** very distinctive—a clearly-defined double note, *tchu-it* or *tchew-eet*, without the ringing musical effect of the Redshank's notes.

Redshank
Tringa totanus

Length: 27 cm
4
Weight: 130–200 g
R

Of all the waders on a marsh the Redshank will often be the most nervous in behaviour, dashing into the air at the least disturbance, with loud, ringing cries which repeatedly set off all the other birds. It is larger than the sandpipers, but much smaller and darker than a godwit. On the ground its medium-length bill and legs and brown coloration are distinctive enough, and the legs are a vivid orange-red (yellower on young birds). In flight the broad white bars on the rear of the wings and its white back and rump make it unmistakable. Flocks gather to roost in hundreds but disperse to feed in widespread groups. **Habitat** wet meadows, salt-marshes, damp moors and bogs; widespread on coasts of all kinds, especially muddy bays and estuaries and adjacent fields. **Nests** on the ground in a long tuft of grass which hides the four eggs laid in April or May. Incubation lasts 22–24 days and the young quickly leave the nest; they fly after about a month. **Food** includes insects, worms, molluscs, even small fish. **Voice** is typically loud and far-carrying, with a ringing quality or yodelling effect. Flight calls are a triple *tyu-hu-hu* and a longer *tyoo*. Alarm notes are a rapid, shouting variation of these. Song is often given in flight, but also from a perch—*tu-udle tu-udle tu-udle* in a long sequence.

Greenshank

Length: 30 cm

4

Tringa nebularia

Weight: 150–250 g

S

Noticeably larger than the Redshank, the Greenshank also has a relatively greater length of bill, neck and legs, giving it an elegance of form that makes it stand out among commoner waders at a reservoir or gravel-pit edge in the autumn. As a breeding bird it is restricted to far northern moors and boggy flows, where it is scarce and widely dispersed. Birds move south early in the autumn and may hang on in winter on a few estuaries. They wade deeply and may dash about like Spotted Redshanks, but are usually quieter in their behaviour. They tend to look very pale and greyish, almost white on the head and neck at times, and very white beneath except for the streaked breast. The bill is stout and slightly upcurved and lacks red; the legs are green or grey-green. In flight the wings are contrastingly dark, with no white bar, but a long triangle of white extends up the back. **Habitat** fresh and salt water edges, but rarely out on open mudflats. Usually ones and twos or small groups in muddy creeks or beside reservoirs if the water level is low. **Nest** on the ground on rolling boggy moors. Four eggs are laid, often close to a rock or stump, and incubated for 24 days. **Food** largely worms, molluscs, small fish. **Voice** a loud and clear *tew tew tew*, lower and less hurried than the Redshank's note.

Green Sandpiper
Tringa ochropus

Length: 22 cm
3

Weight: 70–100 g
M

This wader is very similar to the much rarer **Wood Sandpiper** (*T. glareola*, 20 cm long and weighing 50–90 g), but is stockier and shorter-legged. Both are markedly smaller than a Redshank, but bigger than a Dunlin, with the slender, lightweight appearance of a Common Sandpiper. Green Sandpipers look almost pied, especially in flight, when they dash off at speed, showing a broad white rump but blackish back and wings. The wings are almost as dark below. The Wood Sandpiper is a browner, more boldly chequered bird, with the white rump a little less conspicuous against the paler back, and its underwing is paler. Both species are nervous, active birds; the Green can be seen in spring, but mostly from late summer to late autumn (a few also winter); the Wood is more a late spring and early autumn visitor. **Habitat** Green is found beside water of all sorts—reservoirs, ditches, ponds, salt-marsh creeks. Wood prefers muddy freshwater margins. **Food** insects, worms, seeds. **Voice** Green has a loud and particularly rich, musical *tooeet weet-weet*, often repeated with startling suddenness when flushed; Wood has a thinner, nervous *chip ip ip* or *chiff-iff-iff*.

Common Sandpiper

Actitis hypoleucos

Length: 20 cm

Weight: 40–70 g

3

S

A small, brown and white bird with slim bill and slender bobbing tail, seen beside an upland stream in summer, is likely to be a Common Sandpiper. Elsewhere it is mostly seen in spring and autumn. The upper parts look uniform brown at first, but close views reveal dark mottling on adults and pale notches along the feather edges on juveniles. Otherwise all look brown above and silky white below, the white extending up in front of the bend of the wing and the breast clouded each side with grey-buff. In flight the action is very distinctive and unlike that of any other wader—the wings (which show a long white stripe) are held stiff and slightly arched and beat in a flickering action. **Habitat** clear, rocky or stony streams in upland areas, lochsides, backwaters of fast rivers; in spring and autumn by freshwater of all sorts, salt-marshes. **Nest** on the ground near water. Four large buffish eggs with dark mottles are laid in May or June and incubation lasts 21 days. **Food** largely insects and worms. **Voice** a loud, ringing trill, *twee-wee-wee*, tending to tail off. This is a characteristic sound of the breeding areas and autumn passage sites, sometimes in a loud chorus from groups in the evening. Song is a rapid, rhythmic variation: *kitti-deeit kitti-deeit, kee-wee-didididi* and sharp *tictictictic* notes.

Turnstone

Arenaria interpres

Length: 22 cm

Weight: 80–140 g

3

W/M

This lively little wader is often unseen until it flies ahead along a rocky seashore, perhaps suddenly appearing in a small group which flickers away low over the waves before returning to the rocks farther on. The birds' calls and boldly patterned plumage instantly draw attention; they look nearly black, with white patches on back, rump and wings. In summer plumage (often also seen in spring and autumn) they are a tortoise-shell mixture of black, white and rich chestnut, set off by vivid orange legs. Their short, stout bills are ideally suited for poking about in seaweed and stones, doing just what their name suggests. **Habitat** weedy tide wracks and rocky shores with barnacles and seaweed; also sandier shores with stony or mussel-covered areas. May appear beside waters inland on passage. **Food** mainly molluscs, shrimps, insects and so on, disturbed from beneath the strand-line or amongst growths of seaweed. In a busy feeding action the bird probes from side to side, running ahead half a metre or so or turning back to explore a fresh source of food. **Voice** includes short, sharp notes from feeding groups, which develop into metallic, staccato chattering calls in flight: *kitititit*.

Great Skua

Stercorarius skua

Length: 58 cm

Weight: 1·2–1·4 kg

5

S/M

Skuas are piratical, predatory birds that chase other seabirds and force them to give up, or even disgorge, their catch. Both the Great Skua and the **Arctic Skua** (*S. parasiticus*, 45 cm long and weighing 440 g) breed around the far northern isles and Scottish mainland and occur farther south in spring and autumn. Their respective weights are the best indication of the streamlined, elegant build of the Arctic Skua and the heavy, muscular power of the Great Skua, which can kill smaller birds with ease and is ready to take on even a Gannet. Arctics are largely grey-brown, or dark above and white below with a dusky breastband and a flash of white on the outer wing. Adults have extended central tail feathers. Great Skuas are always all dark brown, streaked and spotted with gingery buff, and have a larger prominent patch of white on the wing. **Habitat** coastal waters, sometimes estuaries and sandy bays; breeding areas are extensive moors and bleak islands. **Nest** on the ground in peaty or heathery areas, often in colonies. **Food** largely fish, small birds, eggs; the Great often steals fish from terns and gulls, the Arctic chiefly from terns and Kittiwakes. Both, but especially the Great, follow boats, taking offal behind them. **Voice** at breeding grounds Arctic has loud, wild wailing cries, *ya-wow, ka-aaoww.* Both are silent at sea.

Great Black-backed Gull

Larus marinus

Length: 65 cm

Weight: 1·5–2 kg

5

R

This giant gull is a magnificent species, the big males
seeming at times to dwarf even Herring Gulls with their
great bulk. They are long and broad in the wing and
masterly, if rather heavy, in flight. In particular, they
look large-headed and heavy-billed, a feature useful in
identifying the less distinctive, mottled brown immatures.
Mature birds are very black above, white on the head,
body and tail, with white spots on the wing-tips. They
have yellow bills with a red spot near the tip, and legs of a
pale, greyish pink. Immatures are more boldly chequered
than other young gulls, with paler heads and large black
bills. **Habitat** coastal cliffs in summer. Otherwise sea
coasts of all kinds, harbours, rubbish tips and reservoirs
inland in winter. **Nest** on a prominent part of a sea cliff.
Three eggs, laid in May, are incubated for 26–28 days; the
young fly after 7–8 weeks. **Food** includes offal from
trawlers, fish, small mammals, garbage, dead animals,
birds. Very predatory at seabird colonies; also often
harries wildfowl in winter. **Voice** strong and deep, but
of the familiar gull pattern—a barking *owk*, *uk-uk-uk*, and
loud wailing calls.

Black-headed Gull

Larus ridibundus

Length: 38 cm

Weight: 250–350 g

4

R

This is generally by far the commonest gull found inland at any time of year. Fields in winter may contain thousands of them. They follow the plough, walk about in search of worms and grubs, chase Lapwings, or simply loaf about before flying off to roost on some lake or reservoir. Many thousands more remain on the coast. In summer they are handsome birds, silvery grey above with a broad triangle of white along the leading edge of the wing, enough to distinguish them at a glance, and a dark brown hood. White eyelids, a deep red bill and plum-red legs complete the breeding season livery. In autumn the hood is soon lost, leaving just a dusky ear spot; the legs turn scarlet, and the bill bright red with a black tip. The white wing-flash identifies them still, as on young birds which have a dark tail-band and dark mottles along the upperwing. The species is active, noisy, highly manoeuvrable and lively. **Habitat** in summer marshes, both salt and fresh, lakes, even tiny peaty moorland pools. Otherwise almost anywhere. **Nests** in colonies on the ground, often in a tussock of rushes; usually three eggs are laid in April or May. Incubation 22–24 days. **Food** small fish, worms, grubs, beetles, seeds, berries, scraps. **Voice** varied, loud and often strident: *kwarr, kik kik, kwup,* etc.

Common Gull

Larus canus

Length: 40 cm

Weight: 370–450 g

4

R

In pattern this bird is much like the larger Herring Gull, but adults have a slightly darker back, with a more prominent white patch on the closed wing at rest, between the grey of the back and the black-and-white wing-tips. The black on the wings is also a little more extensive, as are the white spots. The smaller bill is greenish yellow, with a darker band in winter but never any red, and the legs are grey-green. The head is rounder and noticeably more gentle in expression, with a beady black eye. Young birds are best distinguished by their smaller size and long-winged, elegant shape, fluent flight action with fewer glides, and a broad band of black on the otherwise white tail. Common Gulls are northern birds in the summer but more widespread in winter when they become numerous on some agricultural land and playing fields. **Habitat** moors and coastal areas in summer; in winter seashores, reservoirs and grassy fields. **Nest** on the ground. Three eggs are laid in a grassy nest, and incubated for 24–27 days. Colonies are usually not very large, and not on such high, steep cliffs as those of Herring Gulls. **Food** largely insects, worms; also eggs and chicks. **Voice** higher-pitched and more squealing than the Herring Gull's, including a shrill, screaming *keeee-ya*.

Lesser Black-backed Gull

Larus fuscus

Length: 52 cm

Weight: 600–1000 g

4

R

Lesser Black-backs sometimes look barely half as big as their blacker relatives. They are extremely handsome gulls, with smooth dark grey backs (much paler than the Great's), black-and-white wing-tips and white heads and bodies set off by a deep yellow, red-spotted bill and vivid yellow legs. Compared with the paler Herring Gull they are sleeker, longer-winged and shorter-legged, and show much more dark grey under the wing when overhead. In winter they develop a dark, streaked head and neck (on the Great Black-back these remain white). Young birds are mottled brown, darker than Herring Gulls, with all the flight feathers equally dark. After a year they begin to get dark grey on the back. **Habitat** moors, coastal dunes, islands with dense vegetation, less often cliffs. In winter on shores and around inland tips and reservoirs. **Nest** on the ground, in (sometimes very large) colonies. Lays three eggs in May in a nest of grass and seaweed, and incubates for 26–28 days. **Food** fish, birds, worms, molluscs, eggs, refuse. Often follows ships, going further out to sea than other gulls. **Voice** like the Herring Gull's, but deeper and throatier in quality: *ow-ow-ow, kyow-kyow-kyow* and loud, long wailing calls.

Herring Gull

Larus argentatus

Length: 55 cm

Weight: 750–1200 g

4

R

This is the most familiar large gull, especially beside summer seashores, but also in winter in harbours and at tips inland. Adults have the usual gull pattern of white head and body and a grey back—the grey is pale, sometimes looking bluish or silvery; the wing-tips are black with white spots. The bill is yellow with a red spot, and the legs pink. Young birds are mottled brown, darker on the head than Great Black-backs and paler on wing coverts and inner primaries than young Lesser Black-backs. Many seen inland in winter are larger, darker visitors from Scandinavia. Herring Gulls are some of the most accomplished birds in the air, especially when a stiff breeze lets them exhibit magnificent control above a windswept cliff or beach. **Habitat** seashores; in winter freshwater too, and harbours, tips, playing fields and agricultural land. **Nest** on the ground, more usually on cliffs than the Lesser Black-back, in large, noisy colonies. Increasingly on buildings. Lays three eggs in May in a bulky, grassy nest. Incubates for 25–27 days, the young flying after a further six weeks. **Food** refuse, offal and fish, eggs, shellfish. **Voice** loud and far-carrying, including the familiar seagull squeals and wails, a deep *kyow-yow-yow* and short, barking notes.

Kittiwake
Larus tridactyla

Length: 40 cm
4

Weight: 350–425 g
R

Smaller and slimmer than a Common Gull, the Kittiwake is superficially similar in pattern, but has short black legs, narrow straight-edged wings with the outer part slightly paler than the rest, and wing-tips marked with a black triangle as if dipped in a bottle of ink. Once known, its buoyant flight, angled stance and gentle expression make this bird easy to recognize. Identification is helped by its habit of nesting on tiny ledges on sheer cliffs above the sea; it is an oceanic bird, rare inland. Young birds are also very distinctive, with a black collar, black tail-band and a black W pattern across the upperwings. **Habitat** the open sea, rocky or sandy beaches in summer, sheer cliffs, harbours. Not inland. **Nest** on a ledge, or sometimes on buildings beside docks. Lays two eggs at the end of May and incubates them for 26–28 days. **Food** largely fish, with crustacea, molluscs, worms and offal from trawlers. Feeds from the surface of the sea, or dives into the waves; unlike most gulls, is not a scavenger at the tideline. **Voice** very characteristic at breeding colonies, adding to the atmosphere of the great seabird concentrations around our coasts—a loud, clanging *kitti-way-ake* and variations, and high whining notes.

Sandwich Tern

Sterna sandvicensis

Length: 38 cm

Weight: 210–250 g

4

S

This tern appears rather earlier in spring than the others, often arriving in March. It is a larger, more coarsely built bird, with a shorter tail but long, angled, thin wings. A black bill, tipped with pale yellow, and black legs make it an easy species to identify; at longer range look for the heavy head, front-heavy appearance in flight and extremely pale, silver-grey and white plumage. The forehead becomes white by mid or late summer. Sandwich Terns have the most spectacular plunge dive, hitting the water with a loud smack and sending up a burst of spray. Colonies are often erratic, even large ones sometimes failing to re-establish in some years, or moving elsewhere. **Habitat** offshore waters, particularly in broad bays and off sandy beaches and dunes; this is a sea tern, scarce inland. **Nest** on the ground, on sand or amongst long dune grasses, in dense colonies. Lays 1–2 eggs in May, incubating them for 21–24 days. The young fly after five weeks. **Food** mostly small fish such as sand-eels. **Voice** distinctive in its loud, rasping or grating quality: *kierr-ink* or *kirrick*.

Common Tern

Sterna hirundo

Length: 33 cm

Weight: 100–140 g

4

S

Although grey above and paler below, and a bird of the sea coast and larger areas of freshwater, the Common Tern is easily distinguished from the gulls by its slimmer form, long pointed wings, buoyant and elegant flight and long forked tail.   Adults in summer have a jet black cap, a scarlet bill with a dark tip and red legs.   They are pale grey (not quite white) below, and have darkish streaks near the wing-tips.   These become blacker in the autumn, when the forehead becomes white.   Young birds have some gingery colour about the head and back, a grey rump, white forehead, and pale orange at the base of the bill; their wings are blackish near the front and marked with a grey band at the rear.   **Habitat** sea coasts; lakes, reservoirs and gravel-pits inland.   **Nest** on the ground on rocky or shingly islands, stony beaches, drier parts of salt-marshes.   Three eggs are laid in a hollow, and incubated for 21–28 days; the young fly after about four weeks.   **Food** largely fish, taken from the surface or, most usually, after a steep plunge from the air.   Terns often hover, searching for prey.   **Voice** a variety of short, sharp calls at the colonies, *kit, kikik*; longer, high-pitched, grating notes sound like an emphatic *keee-yaah*.

Arctic Tern

Sterna paradisaea

Length: 35 cm

Weight: 80–110 g

4

S

A summer visitor and passage migrant, the Arctic Tern has one of the longest migrations in the bird world—some breed far to the north in the Arctic, and they spend the winter in the Antarctic. The pattern of an adult is almost exactly like that of the Common Tern, but the under parts are greyer, the rump purer white and the wings pale grey and unmarked, looking cleaner above. The underwing is whiter, with a much thinner line of dark along the trailing edge. The bill is all deep red; the legs extremely short. Young birds have all-dark bills, little or no buff tinge above, pure white rumps and wings with a white triangle at the back. In flight the Arctic Tern looks even lighter, longer-winged, shorter-necked and rounder-headed than the Common Tern. **Habitat** a more northerly bird than the Common; rocky sea coasts, sandy beaches and offshore waters. Occurs inland on passage, sometimes many moving quickly through in spring. **Nest** on the ground, in colonies. Lays two eggs in late May or June. Eggs hatch after 22 days, and young fly a month later. **Food** mostly fish, caught in vertical plunge. **Voice** much as that of Common Tern: *pee-airr*, *keeyaah*, and a high, rising *kee kee*.

Little Tern

Sterna albifrons

Length: 25 cm

Weight: 50–60 g

3

S

This tiny tern, with its rapid, flickering wingbeats and movements much jerkier than those of the larger species, is best distinguished, apart from size, by its yellow bill and legs. Also, even in full breeding plumage, the forehead of an adult is white, above a black line. The outer wing feathers are blackish on top. Young birds are dowdier, tinged grey-brown, with blackish bill and legs. They too have a rapid flight action, often sweeping up to hover above the breakers before plunging into the surf. Like other terns they arrive in spring and leave in late autumn, often gathering in sizeable concentrations before they go. They are, however, scarcer than Common or Arctic Terns and their continued survival depends upon special protective measures. **Habitat** sandy and shingly beaches and adjacent offshore waters. Scarce inland. **Nest** on the ground, usually amongst pebbles and often very close to the tideline. Eggs and young are often washed out by high tides or stormy seas. The 2–3 eggs are incubated for 19–22 days, and the young fly after four weeks. **Food** very largely small fish. **Voice** a quick, chattering version of that of other terns, including *kik-kik*, *kyik*, and a distinctive, fast *kirrikiki kirrikiki*.

Guillemot
Uria aalge

Length: 41 cm

4

Weight: 900–1100 g

R

A little larger, but slimmer in build than the Razorbill, the Guillemot is nevertheless much the same in its habits and general appearance. In flight at a distance, when both birds race along with whirring wingbeats, looking heavy, and tapered abruptly each end, the two are hard to tell apart. In summer, at a closer range, the Guillemot is decidedly browner (southern ones can look pale chocolate in sunlight); it has a thinner, more pointed bill. Colonies are sometimes very large, and huge rafts of the birds gather on the sea beneath the sheer nesting cliffs, with scores more flying in and out, adding to the ever-fascinating hustle and bustle of the big seabird cities. **Habitat** the open sea, offshore waters; sheer cliffs. **Nest** on horizontal ledges, often very narrow, the birds closely packed together, often above Kittiwakes. Its one egg, laid in late May, is incubated for 28–36 days and the chick flutters to the sea after only 15–20 days. **Food** largely fish, taken underwater, but also crustacea and molluscs. **Voice** at colonies, chiefly loud whirring notes which rise and fall in remarkable choruses from the ledges—*aarrrr.*

Razorbill
Alca torda

Length: 40 cm
4

Weight: 550–750 g
R

The auks, of which this is one, are birds of the open sea, coming to land only to breed, although the Razorbill tends to frequent sheltered bays and estuaries more than do the Guillemot or Puffin. It is the bulkiest of the three (although the Guillemot is larger), black above and white below. In summer the throat is black, but in winter the foreneck and lower face are white, below a black cap. A white line runs forward from each eye, and the deep flattened bill is crossed by a pale band. The Razorbill has a pointed tail (unlike the square tail of the browner Guillemot), often held cocked clear of the water as it swims. **Habitat** the sea; rocky and cliff-bound shores. **Nest** in a cavity or crevice, or amongst broken boulders, less on open cliff ledges; colonial and frequently mixed with those of Guillemots and Kittiwakes. Lays one egg in late May; the chick hatches after 33–36 days and leaves the ledge after 18 days, long before it is able to fly. **Food** largely fish, shrimps, shellfish. Dives from surface and swims underwater. **Voice** includes grating growls and whirring sounds—*caarrr, wu-urrrr.*

Black Guillemot

Cepphus grylle

Length: 33 cm

Weight: 350–450 g

4

R

Unlike our other auks, the Black Guillemot in summer is all sooty black beneath, having white only in one very conspicuous patch on each wing. The legs and the inside of the mouth (often visible as a bird calls) are vivid red. Young birds and adults in winter are very different, being white below and mottled black and white all over the head, neck and upper parts; the white wing patch remains a useful feature. Black Guillemots are smaller than Guillemots, far less abundant, and quieter, more sober in behaviour, spending long periods in sheltered bays and inlets between rocky headlands, diving frequently or simply loafing about. **Habitat** rocky coasts and islands, inshore waters. A bird of the far north and west. **Nest** in small groups, not big colonies, in cliff crevices or cavities amongst boulders. Lays two eggs in May. **Food** includes small fish, marine worms, shellfish, shrimps. Feeds, like other auks, by diving underwater from the surface. **Voice** often heard from birds near nest from cliff or water, a shrill whistle, *peeeeeee*, which may run into a trill.

Puffin
Fratercula arctica

Length: 30 cm
4

Weight: 350–450 g
R

On rocky islands that have slopes of short, rabbit-grazed grass, clumps of pink thrift and sea campion and wheeling gulls overhead, the scene may well be completed by the Puffins which gather in rafts offshore and come in to nest in burrows in the turf. They are black and white, with bright orange legs; the grey face, surrounded in black, has a magnificent bill, deep and triangular and banded with red, yellow and blue-grey. Often tame and confiding, and fascinating to watch, Puffins are amongst the most attractive of all our birds. In winter, should one by chance be seen close to the shore, it might confuse an observer not prepared for its dowdier appearance, dark face and much smaller, nondescript bill. The Puffin's flight is like that of other auks, but its wings seem even smaller and whirr still more rapidly. **Habitat** the open sea. Comes to breed on cliffs and islands, especially those with grassy tracts, and soil into which it can burrow. **Nests** in a hole. The one egg is incubated for 40–43 days, and the young bird does not leave the nest for another 50 days or so. **Food** mostly fish, taken by swimming underwater. **Voice** in or around the burrows or on the sea nearby is a growling *arr*.

Rock Dove

Columba livia

Length: 34 cm

Weight: 250–300 g

4

R

The wild, native Rock Dove is the ancestor of domestic pigeons, some of which, having gone back to live in the wild, are called feral pigeons or feral Rock Doves. These include the big flocks of central London and other cities, but they are also widespread in quarries, industrial areas and on inland and coastal cliffs. On the cliffs they mix with the wild Rock Doves and tend to blur the true characteristics of the original type. Feral pigeons are all sorts of colours and patterns, but Rock Doves are blue-grey, very pale above, with an iridescent patch on the neck, a whitish underwing, two black bars across each wing and a big white patch on the lower back. They are swift, dashing pigeons, ideally suited to the roaring winds and swirling updraughts of their wild seaside haunts. **Habitat** cliffs on the coast; farmland miles inland along valleys; islands. Feral birds almost anywhere. **Nest** in caves or on a cliff ledge. Two eggs are laid in April or later. Incubation lasts 17–19 days. **Food** grain, roots, leaves and seeds, and various vegetable crops. **Voice** just like that of dovecote pigeons, a crooning *oor-roo-cooo*.

Stock Dove

Columba oenas

Length: 34 cm

Weight: 300–500 g

4

R

Typically a pigeon in looks, the Stock Dove is best identified by its overall blue-grey colour, with the tips and trailing edge of the wing blacker, and an iridescent green patch on the neck. It has no white on wing or neck, nor the white underwing which many domestic pigeons show. It is smaller, neater and rounder-headed than the Woodpigeon. It may occur in large flocks, but is generally less numerous than the latter species. Although best known, perhaps, as a bird of farmland and parks, it is equally at home on a cliff, either high inland or on the coast. **Habitat** woods, parkland with old trees, agricultural land, cliffs. **Nest** in holes in trees, in a cliff cavity, the ledge of an old barn, or in a rabbit burrow. Lays two eggs from March onwards, with at least two broods. Incubation lasts 16–18 days and the young fly after four weeks. **Food** mostly vegetable matter—grain, seeds, green leaves, roots, berries. **Voice** deep and rhythmic, with the second syllable short and abrupt: *ooo-woo*. This song is heard mostly from February to July.

Woodpigeon
Columba palumbus

Length: 40 cm
4

Weight: 400–550 g
R

This is a big, heavy pigeon, with long wings and tail and a deep, curved breast. In flight from a perch it is amazingly swift and agile, sideslipping and twisting through branches and bushes until reaching clear air where it can speed away in direct, powerful movement. A close view shows it to be a beautiful soft blue-grey, browner on the back, with a deep pinkish breast. The sides of the neck are purple and green; the tail banded dark and pale grey. Identification is made easy by the broad band of white across each black-tipped wing and (except in juveniles) the white patch on each side of the neck. Always sociable, Woodpigeons may form into flocks of thousands in autumn and winter, hated by farmers but a marvellous feature of the landscape. **Habitat** farmland near woods, parkland, conifer and deciduous woods and plantations; also dunes, rough grassy areas above cliffs, salt-marshes. **Nest** in a tall hedge or tree, also on rocks or buildings. Lays two eggs mainly from July to September; incubation lasts 17–19 days. Two broods. **Voice** the familiar crooning song, typically *coo-cooo, coo, coo-coo*. It is like other pigeons in having no alarm or contact notes, but its wings are clapped in display and make a loud clatter as the bird takes off.

Collared Dove

Streptopelia decaocto

Length: 31 cm

Weight: 150–200 g

4

R

A resident (unlike the Turtle Dove), and much more likely to be seen in and around gardens, farmyards and urban areas, this is a larger, duller bird.   In flight its tail shows, from below, much more white at the end, and on top does not have the Turtle Dove's prominent white-rimmed area of black.   The head and under parts are pale pinkish-brown, the upper parts grey-brown, giving a pale fawn or greyish appearance depending on the light.   The wing-tips are dark and across the spread wing is a band of blue-grey, but there is no strong pattern except for a thin half-collar of black across the back of the neck.   It is a bird that associates itself with human habitation, especially where there is grain to be found.   **Habitat** parks, gardens, factory estates, railway yards, chicken runs, distilleries, etc.   **Nest** in a tree such as a dense ornamental conifer; lays two eggs from March onwards.   Incubation lasts 14 days and the young fly after three weeks.   Two or more broods.   **Food** largely spilled grain, berries, seeds and scraps.   **Voice** includes an alarm and flight note (unusual for our pigeons)—a nasal *kwurr*.   Song is loud and monotonous with the third note abrupt: *coo-coooo-cuk*.

Turtle Dove

Streptopelia turtur

Length: 27 cm

Weight: 100–150 g

3

S

Summer days with warm sun and hedgerows in blossom provide the best setting for the purring song of the Turtle Dove. It is a summer visitor. Of our doves and pigeons it is the smallest, most delicate and most attractively patterned—although it lacks the bold contrasts of the Woodpigeon, showing its subtle colouring only in a close view. The upper parts are largely pale brown, with blackish feather centres forming a regular pattern; the head and neck are grey, the breast pale pink. The outer wing is very dark, but across the coverts is a pale blue-grey band; much more obvious as it flies is the tail, which is black except for white edges and a broad white band at the tip. The flight is fast, with whippy wingbeats. **Habitat** parkland, open woods with thickets, clumps of trees and hawthorns on heathland, tall bushy hedges. Often perches on wires beside roads and around fields of grain. **Nest** in a tall bush or thick hedge; it lays two eggs from May onwards, with a second brood later. Incubation is for only 13–14 days, and the young fly within three weeks. **Food** vegetable matter, seeds, berries and leaves of all sorts. **Voice** an even, purring note, *rrooorrrr rrooorrrr.*

Cuckoo
Cuculus canorus

Length: 33 cm
4

Weight: 100–140 g
S

From April to July Cuckoos are a prominent part of the countryside and its birdlife. After that, the males cease to call and adults migrate back to Africa, leaving only the juveniles which stay until September. The adult is a grey bird, with white spots near the tip of the long, dark tail. Underneath it is paler, with a grey breast but lower down has grey bars on a whitish background. In flight it shows long, broad-based wings which curve back and taper to a point. The grey colour, curved wings and broad-tipped, rounded tail distinguish it from a Kestrel; Sparrowhawks are quite different in shape, while Merlins are much quicker, narrower in the tail and lack the white spots. Young Cuckoos have rounder wings; they are brown, and heavily barred, with a pale spot at the back of the head. **Habitat** woodland, heaths, farmland with hedges, reedy swamps, moorland. Does not build a nest, but lays eggs singly in nests of other species such as the Meadow Pipit, Dunnock and Reed Warbler. Incubation lasts 12½ days and the chick flies after three weeks. **Food** mostly insects and spiders, also hairy caterpillars. **Voice** the familiar *coo-coo*, occasionally *cuc-cuc-coo* from the male; hoarse chuckling notes and a rich bubbling trill from the female.

Barn Owl
Tyto alba

Length: 36 cm
4

Weight: 250–350 g
R

Widespread, but now generally rather scarce, the Barn Owl is perhaps most often seen hunting beside roads, either on a winter's afternoon, or picked out as a white shape by a car's headlights. Although chiefly nocturnal, it may be seen out early in the evening if it has young to feed, or if hard pressed by harsh weather. Few birds are more attractive when seen clearly. The under parts and underwings are white; the face white with dark marks near the eyes and framing a heart-shaped disk; the upper parts pale buff or richer, golden-buff, the flight feathers paler but barred with grey. In flight it looks big-headed but slightly short-winged; nevertheless, the action is buoyant and wavering, with short hovers before a plunge into grass after prey. The dive after a mouse is often head first into soft vegetation. **Habitat** fields and open country, marshes; close to old trees, barns, ruins. **Nest** in a building such as a barn or church; in hollow trees or a hole in a cliff. Lays 4–7 eggs in April or May; they hatch after 32–34 days and the young fly after 9–10 weeks. **Food** mostly small rodents; also birds, beetles. **Voice** includes a long shriek; a quick *ik-ik-ik*, and various hissing and snoring noises.

Little Owl
Athene noctua

Length: 23 cm
3

Weight: 150–200 g
R

A small, dumpy, flat-headed bird, dark liver-brown with pale spots above, more streaked beneath, this is one of the owls most frequently seen in southern Britain. Although it does not hunt by day, it sits out in the open in the daytime, and is often discovered by small birds which mob it noisily, and help its location by birdwatchers. Often it allows a close approach, but bobs and twists its head as it examines the intruder. Close views reveal its fierce expression, with pale brows low over the bright yellow eyes. If it should fly, it does so with a rapid action, bursts of quick wingbeats alternating with spurts with closed wings to give a noticeably bounding effect. **Habitat** farmland with tall hedges and scattered trees; lines of pollarded willows; open, rocky country near the coast. England and Wales only. **Nest** in a tree hole, rabbit burrow, or a cavity in a cliff or rocky slope. Lays 3–5 eggs in April or May, which hatch after 28 days. The young fly after 35–40 days. **Food** largely beetles and other large insects, with birds, small mammals, worms and even frogs at times. **Voice** far-carrying, usually a loud, clear *kiew* or *kee-yooo*.

Tawny Owl
Strix aluco

Length: 37 cm
4

Weight: 400–650 g
R

Although this is generally by far our commonest owl (but absent in Ireland and some outer islands), it is difficult to see except as a shadowy figure at night in a town park or suburban area with well-wooded gardens. If calling birds can be tracked down, or a daytime roost found, then it can be watched more regularly. It is a big owl, with a very large, round head. The plumage is usually a rich, warm brown, with a row of creamy spots either side of the back, and streaks of brown on buff below. The eyes are black. In flight it is a short, broad-winged bird, with a small tail but very heavy head. **Habitat** principally woods, but often parks, churchyards, gardens with big, dense trees. **Nest** in hole in tree, an old squirrel's drey, or a disused nest. Lays 2–4, or more, eggs in March or April; they are incubated for 28–30 days. The young leave the nest after about five weeks; often only one or two survive, depending upon the supply of food. **Food** voles, mice, rats, small birds; many worms and beetles. **Voice** includes the well-known (but often misquoted) hooting song after dark—*hoo-hoo, oo* followed by a long, wavering *hooooooo*. The sharp *kewick* (or *tu-whit*) is given separately. This latter note, with loud and nasal variations and squalling sounds, is given by young birds.

Short-eared Owl

Asio flammeus

Length: 37 cm

Weight: 270–350 g

4

R

Compared with a Tawny Owl, the Short-eared is just as long, and much longer in the wing, but more lightly built and far less bulky.   It is a paler, more buff-brown owl, far less reddish, with silvery-white under parts streaked with black, and a boldly mottled upperside.   In flight, the strong pattern on the upperwing is obvious; it comprises a white leading edge, a row of white spots along the coverts, a white trailing edge, and at the bend of the wing a dark brown patch inside a wider area of orange-buff or cream.   Clear yellow eyes glow from black-rimmed sockets.   Such details can often be seen because the bird hunts in daylight.   **Habitat** open ground over which it can fly slowly at low level—rough pasture, marshes, moors, young conifer plantations.   Absent from Ireland.   May occur in small groups where voles are abundant. **Nest** on the ground, amongst heather, rushes or gorse.   Lays 4–8 eggs, and incubates them for 24–28 days.   The young fly after about four weeks.   **Food** largely voles, some small birds.   **Voice** a harsh, wheezing *sch-wair*, a deep bark and a quick, deep, hollow *boo-boo-boo*.   Also makes a rapid slapping sound by clapping its wings beneath the body during display flight.

Swift
Apus apus

Length: 16 cm
2

Weight: 35–45 g
S

Flickering wings propel the Swift through the air at high speed, whether it is shooting between houses in screaming groups, feeding high in the sky on a fine day, or forced in bad weather to hunt for insects low over a lake or reservoir. Unlike the Swallow and the martins, it looks black all over unless close enough to reveal its sooty brown coloration, with a dull white throat. It also has longer, more slender, more sickle-shaped wings than any of the other aerial feeders. The swift *never* perches on wires, aerials or roofs. It is with us from May to September. **Habitat** in the air over all sorts of country, but especially over villages and suburbs with houses suitable for nesting. **Nest** in colonies, under the eaves of older houses; in a few places in natural crevices. The 2–3 eggs laid at the end of May are incubated for 18–20 days; the young fly after about six weeks, and then may not come back to rest for three years! **Food** entirely insects taken on the wing. **Voice** usually a long, harsh scream or screech, often in noisy chorus from a flock chasing around the colony.

Kingfisher
Alcedo atthis

Length: 16 cm
2

Weight: 35–45 g
R

Smaller than many people expect, the Kingfisher is hard to see despite its bright colours. Somehow the bright rusty-orange, white and blue seem to disappear amongst the vegetation and reflections where it perches above a rippling stream or clear lake. The plop of a bird diving in for a fish is often the first indication that it is there. The shrill call is also an excellent clue to its presence. A good view reveals the finery of its iridescent blue upper parts. In flight the stumpy form, almost tail-less, but long billed, with a streak of lightning blue down the back, leaves no doubt as to its identity—but it may then go right off out of sight leaving the watcher disappointed! **Habitat** fresh water of all kinds, and rocky seashores; in the winter muddy gutters in marshes, etc. **Nest** in a steep bank, usually above water. Digs a tunnel, in which 6–7 eggs are laid. They hatch after 19–21 days and the young fly at between 3–4 weeks old. Two broods are reared. **Food** mostly small fish, but also tadpoles and water insects. **Voice** a loud, shrill *chee* or *chikee*, which may develop into a trilling song.

Green Woodpecker
Picus viridis

Length: 32 cm
4

Weight: 170–200 g
R

If flushed unexpectedly from the ground on an open heath, or from the ant-hills in a meadow, the bright yellow rump and green upperside of this large bird may take one by surprise. A woodpecker is, perhaps, not to be expected in the open—but this species is often a ground-feeder. The red crown and fast, bounding flight confirm the identification suggested by the bright rump. In trees, even if it is calling, such a large bird can be difficult to locate, when hanging motionless from a branch amongst the greenery. Young birds have more grey in the red crown, and streaks and bars over the neck and breast. **Habitat** open broad-leaved woods and parks, heaths, dunes. Rarely in coniferous or dense woods. Not in Ireland. **Nest** in a hole which it bores into the trunk of a tree. Lays 5–7 eggs, which are incubated for 15–17 days. The young fly after three weeks. **Food** chiefly the larvae of insects which bore into wood, and ants taken from their nest with the bird's long, sticky tongue. **Voice** loud and clear, with a nasal or squeaky quality: *kew kew kew kewkewkew*, or a sharper *kewkewkew*. Drums (by hammering its bill against a branch) only very rarely.

Great Spotted Woodpecker
Dendrocopos major

Length: 23 cm
3

Weight: 75–83 g
R

This is the lively, relatively common woodpecker of both deciduous and coniferous woods in Britain. It clings to the side of a branch or tree-trunk, tapping with its bill and probing for grubs. It makes short, jerky hops or leaps from branch to branch, before moving on with typical bounding, undulating flight. The black-and-white plumage, tinged buff beneath and set off by a blaze of red under the tail, is always distinctive. Males have a red spot on the nape. (The **Lesser Spotted Woodpecker**, *D. minor*), a much scarcer species, is only as big as a sparrow and spends its time amongst the thinner twigs. It lacks the broad white shoulder patches of the Great Spotted, looking barred instead.) **Habitat** woods, orchards, wooded gardens. **Nest** in a hole dug out from a tree-trunk or stout branch. Lays 4–7 eggs in May; after 16 days the young hatch, to fly 18–21 days later. **Food** mainly grubs of wood-boring insects; spiders; sometimes nestling birds. **Voice** distinctive once learnt—a loud, penetrating *tchick*. Also a rattling call. Drums with its bill against wood, producing a very short, vibrant burst of hollow sound.

Skylark
Alauda arvensis

Length: 18 cm
2

Weight: 30–50 g
R

A bird of open terrain, the Skylark normally lacks branches or other song posts. It therefore flies vertically up into the sky as it sings. This behaviour is its most notable feature. A close view reveals a complex pattern of buff and brown, with a broad band of streaky buff across the chest contrasting with off-white under parts. The bill is fairly stout; the head has a short crest. In flight it shows a trailing edge of white on each wing and white sides to the short tail. Larger than finches, sparrows and pipits, it is of similar bulk to the Corn Bunting. In winter Skylarks may gather into flocks scattered over open fields or crops, and hard weather causes large-scale daytime movements to the west. **Habitat** open grassland, dunes, bogs, moorland, cultivated fields. Avoids trees. **Nest** on the ground. Lays 3–4 eggs from April onwards, and incubation lasts 11 days, the young flying after 20 days. Two or three broods. **Food** includes seeds, small worms, insects. **Voice** a trilling or rippling *chirrup* as it takes flight, a thin *see* from flocks in the air, and the famous long, loud song, poured out from the air (or a rare perch), often unbroken for minutes on end. The rich warbling song tends to sound higher pitched and silvery from a distance or at a great height.

Sand Martin
Riparia riparia

Length: 12 cm
I

Weight: 12–18 g
S

This is the smallest of the swallows and martins, and the only one which is obviously brown on top with no white (but white underneath, with a brown band across the chest). The Sand Martin is also less frequently seen about houses and buildings. It appears earlier in the spring than the others, often in March, but numbers have generally declined in recent years because of adverse conditions in its African winter-quarters. It has a weaker, more fluttery flight than that of the House Martin, its slender wings flexed well back and flickered in and out. Although very much an aerial bird, it frequently perches on wires. **Habitat** often near water, especially early in the spring and again in the autumn, when large numbers may mix with Swallows to roost in reeds. **Nest** in holes dug into sand-banks in quarries, gravel-pits or on riversides. The 4–5 eggs hatch after 14 days. The young fly at 19 days old. There are often two broods. **Food** insects, caught on the wing. **Voice** is rippling or chirruping, with a harder, more chattering quality than that of the Swallow. It is developed into a chattering song.

Swallow
Hirundo rustica

Length: 18 cm
2

Weight: 16–25 g
S

This popular bird has a most elegant, swooping flight as it searches for insects not far above the ground. (The Swift and House Martin typically feed higher up.) The Swallow is always distinguished by its completely dark blue upper parts (except for white spots in the tail), combined with pale, often pinkish-buff under parts (except for a dark throat). In a close view the chin and forehead can be seen to be deep red. Few birds have such elegance of form combined with such attractive coloration. Old males have very long tail streamers, which are shorter on females and quite stubby on young birds, which are coloured much as adults. **Habitat** open country, especially near water. Often close to farmsteads and outbuildings where it can nest. **Nest** on rafters in sheds or huts of some sort, needing access through an open door or window. Lays 4–5 eggs, which hatch after 14–15 days; the young fly when three weeks old. Usually two broods. **Food** entirely insects taken on the wing, often over lawns, tennis courts, etc, or over water. **Voice** includes a soft, twittering *tswit tswitwit*, and a pleasant warbling and twittering song with a low, churring trill.

House Martin
Delichon urbica

Length: 13 cm
2

Weight: 15–20 g
S

With its more fluttery, less swooping flight, pure white under parts and a broad band of white across the rump, the House Martin is easily distinguished from the Swallow. It is more familiar in small towns and housing estates, although absent from the larger cities, where insects are not to be found. It tends to feed at a higher level than the Swallow, often over houses. Like the Swallow purely a summer visitor, it is here only from April to October. **Habitat** varied, nesting on houses, under bridges or on new buildings of all sorts and not restricted to open sheds and outbuildings as is the Swallow. **Nest** on the wall of a building beneath the eaves or a beam, making the well-known cup of mud with a hole at the top. Lays 4–5 eggs, which are incubated by both sexes for two weeks. After three weeks the young fly; there may be two or three broods. **Food** entirely insects taken in flight. **Voice** is less soft and slurred than the Swallow's, more of a chirrup or chirp, with a far less frequent twittering song.

Tree Pipit
Anthus trivialis

Length: 15 cm
2

Weight: 20–25 g
S

So much like the Meadow Pipit that it is best distinguished by voice, the Tree Pipit at least helps identification by being a summer visitor to Britain—so it can be ruled out from October to March! It looks a little cleaner and neater than the Meadow Pipit, is slightly more solidly built, and has a shorter hind claw (a useful feature). Its upper parts are browner, its under parts clear buff, and it shows a larger area of clean, almost unmarked flank. Meadow pipits may perch in trees, but a pipit seen walking about on tree branches is likely to be this one. **Habitat** tall tree belts on edges of woodland and of felled plantations, and between farmland and moors; rough ground with bushes and trees. **Nest** on the ground; 4–6 eggs are laid in May or June and hatch after 13–14 days. The young fly in just 12–13 days' time. **Food** largely insects and spiders. **Voice** the call is a buzzy or grating *tzee* or *teez* (quite unlike the Meadow Pipit's sharper, more musical note). The song has richer notes, especially rolling trills, and often ends in a series of loud, sweet, long *swee swee swee* calls. It is a long phrase, but not so prolonged or varied as is a Skylark's song. The song flight starts and finishes on a high perch.

Meadow Pipit

Anthus pratensis

Length: 15 cm

Weight: 18–22 g

2

R

Although a resident, the Meadow Pipit is in effect a winter visitor to much of the lowlands, and an early summer visitor to the moors where it nests. It is a small, slim bird, with a bit of wagtail about it in its shape and quick, running actions. Most birds are a bright olive-brown, softly streaked darker above, and creamy buff with sharp dark streaks beneath; but some look greyer, some greener. All have a dark tail with pure white sides which show well as they fly up, a few yards ahead, bounce upwards for a few seconds, then quickly drop back to earth. More often than not, they call as they go. **Habitat** open country— moors, commons, rough ground by the sea; in winter cultivated country, waste ground, marshes. Often beside water. **Nest** on the ground. The 4–5 eggs hatch after two weeks' incubation and the young fly after a further two weeks or so. **Food** largely insects, spiders, odd seeds. **Voice** a thin, squeaky, but sharply uttered *tseep*, often repeated several times as the bird takes flight; and a shorter *sip*. The song is given in a special rising song flight, which finishes with a steep 'parachute' back to the ground. It comprises a long, thin, tinkling series of short *sip* notes, quickening into more of a trill and fading away.

Rock Pipit

Anthus spinoletta

Length: 16 cm

Weight: 22–26 g

R

This, the largest of our common pipits, is virtually restricted to the coast, but a few birds appear beside reservoirs inland in spring and autumn. It looks a slightly heavier, and noticeably duller bird than the Meadow Pipit. It is a greyer olive above, with smudgy, dusky streaking, yellower below, with broad, diffuse streaking all over. The legs, unlike those of the other pipits, are very dark. The outer tail feathers also look dull, not bright white. **Habitat** seaside areas—rocky shores and islets, cliffs and beaches; marshes and muddy creeks in winter. **Nest** in a cavity in a cliff or rocky bank. The 4–5 eggs take 14 days to hatch and the young fly after 16 days. Two broods. **Food** mostly insects, small shoreline creatures, a few seeds. **Voice** a fuller, more slurred version of the Meadow Pipit's: more like *feest*. The song, often given in a song flight above the rocks, is in pattern also like the Meadow Pipit's, but louder and more musical.

The **Water Pipit**, a race of the Rock Pipit (or a closely related species), occurs in winter on muddy shores and freshwater edges. It also has dark legs, but is dull white beneath, with narrower streaking; it has a broad pale superciliary and pale wing-bars.

Yellow Wagtail

Length: 17 cm

2

Motacilla flava

Weight: 16–20 g

S

Present from April to September, mainly in England, this lively, long-striding little bird is best sought near still or slow-flowing water, in wet meadows or on close-cropped turf. It often attracts attention by its call, or flies on ahead in a series of undulations, to settle again with bobbing tail and an inquisitive air. Small groups are frequent, and spring and autumn flocks may be a hundred strong; but their association is rather loose, they do not bunch together like finches. Essentially ground birds, they rarely enter trees, but do roost in reeds or long grass. Males are vivid yellow beneath and green above, with dark wings crossed by two white bars. Females are duller, and young ones have dark marks on the chest. The black tail with white edges is obvious. **Habitat** water-meadows, reservoir edges and riversides; often amongst cattle. **Nest** on the ground. Lays one or two clutches of 5–6 eggs. **Food** mainly insects taken from the ground or in short flycatching sallies. **Voice** a loud, shrill note, sounding like *tsweep*. Song is a simple warbling, with this call intermixed.

Grey Wagtail
Motacilla cinerea

Length: 18 cm
2

Weight: 17–23 g
R

The Grey Wagtail is even more slender than the Pied Wagtail, and very long-tailed. All Grey Wagtails have a patch of vivid yellow under the tail (they are thus often mistaken for Yellow Wagtails, which are summer visitors, whereas the Grey is resident all the year). On top they are soft blue-grey, with a thin white stripe over the eye, and a yellowish rump. Underneath, spring males have a black chin and yellow under parts; the females are duller. In winter all birds are a pale, dingy buff. The tail is black, with white sides. Grey Wagtails are very much associated with water. **Habitat** in summer, upland streams, with or without trees, often fast-flowing and rocky. At other times, lakes and reservoirs, even pools on flat roofs, or car-parks. **Nest** in a hole or a cavity in a bank or amongst tree roots. The 4–6 eggs are incubated for 14 days and the young fly after just 12 days. **Food** mostly insects, caught from the water's edge, on rocks or taken in the air. **Voice** similar to that of the Pied Wagtail, but higher in pitch and much sharper: *tsik* or *tissik*. The song is a thin, buzzy twitter, sometimes more developed.

Pied Wagtail
Motacilla alba

Length: 18 cm
2

Weight: 20–25 g
R

A common, sprightly bird, with thin black legs and a long, sometimes bobbing tail, the Pied Wagtail is easily identified. Juveniles have a buffish face but little of the real yellow colour shown by Yellow and Grey Wagtails. Adult females are greyish on the back, with a black and white face, black throat, and a black tail with white sides. The spring males, with jet black back, sooty flanks and broad black chest patch are quite unmistakeable. Pied Wagtails do perch (and often roost) in trees, but they are principally birds of the ground, chasing after flies or flying up to catch them in mid-air. **Habitat** very varied—from flat roofs, car-parks and metalled footpaths to open, moorland country, riversides, damp meadows, gravel-pits, wood yards, etc. **Nest** in a hole in a wall or bank, in a wood-pile or on a ledge. The 5–6 eggs hatch after 14 days and the young fly after 14–16 days. **Food** largely insects. **Voice** includes two characteristic calls: a loud hard *tchissik* and a bright loud, more musical *chuwee*. Song, not often heard, is a varied twittering warble, with or without the *chuwee* note intermixed.

Dipper
Cinclus cinclus

Length: 18 cm

3

Weight: 60–70 g

R

This stocky, strong little bird with its frequent springy bobbing action, is well camouflaged, in black, brown and white, for its waterside environment. It stands on a rock or a shingle bank beside a stream, or perches in a riverside tree, and is surprisingly hard to pick out. The Dipper is remarkable and unique amongst small birds in being able to dive from the water's surface or from the air, or to walk into the water, disappearing underneath even in a flow so rough and fast that one expects it to be carried away downstream. But it pops up again at the place where it dived in, after walking about on the bottom of the stream quite at home in the torrent. **Habitat** the edges of rivers and streams, often in the hills, but also beside broader, quieter streams with well-wooded banks. **Nest** under an overhanging rock, even beneath a waterfall, or under a bridge, making a large untidy nest with a side entrance. Lays about five eggs which hatch after 16 days. The young, which are paler than adults, fly after 19–25 days. Two broods. **Food** aquatic insects, molluscs, tadpoles, small fish. **Voice** a loud, flat *zit zit*. Also a long, rambling, warbling song.

Wren

Troglodytes troglodytes

Length: 10 cm
I

Weight: 8–12 g
R

The Wren's tiny size, its usually cocked tail, and its barred rusty-brown colour make it easy to identify. But it is often difficult to see, because it loves to explore deep in undergrowth or under the darkest overhangs in ditches and hedge banks. It is not, however, particularly shy, and is as likely to sit up in full view and chatter noisily when disturbed as to slip silently away. It is not a visitor to bird-tables, and rarely takes food put out for birds; but wrens do use nest-boxes for roosting in winter. **Habitat** very varied—from high moors to lowland woods, heaths, gardens, hedges; rocky coastal regions, cliffs, islands. **Nest** under an overhang in a low bank, in a hedge or an outbuilding, making a round grassy nest with a side entrance. Lays 5–6 eggs from April onwards; they hatch after 14 days and the young fly when 16–17 days old. Normally two broods. **Food** largely insects and spiders. **Voice** shrill and clear and particularly loud and explosive. A rattling *tik tik tik*, often developing into a chatter; and a loud, fast warbling song with a churring trill towards the end.

Dunnock
Prunella modularis

Length: 15 cm
2

Weight: 20–24 g
R

For one of the common-est and most widespread birds of Britain, the Dun-nock is very much over-looked and neglected. Although it is very com-mon in gardens, it is not a bird-table or nest-box bird—in fact it gets on very nicely without us. It is very adaptable, equally at home on a heathery moor or above some sea cliff. The Dunnock is a small, slightly sparrow-like bird. It has rich brown upper parts streaked with black, a grey head with no black on it, and under parts with soft streaks of brown. Instead of the stout beak of a sparrow, it has a thin, insect-eater's bill. Note, too, its orange legs as the bird shuffles quietly about the shrubbery or in the bottom of a hedge. **Habitat** gardens, woodland edges, hedge-rows, scrubby areas. **Nest** in a hedge or bush; lays 4–5 eggs from April onwards. They hatch after 12–13 days and the young leave the nest after only 12 days. **Food** mostly seeds in winter; and insects, spiders, etc, in the summer. **Voice** includes a loud, high *tseep*, often heard but ignored. The song is a bright, quick but slightly flat warble, with neither the best songsters' richness nor the Wren's vehemence. It is a phrase repeated at intervals, with little variation.

Robin
Erithacus rubecula

Length: 16 cm
2

Weight: 18–20 g
R

The red-breasted Robin, so tame and confiding with man, so aggressive to others of its species, round and dumpy and shown on millions of Christmas cards, hardly needs description. Young ones, however, are brown and mottled all over with spots of buff. Their shape and perky actions combined with their brown (not rufous) tail should distinguish them from the similarly mottled young Redstarts and Nightingales. Robins become shy and skulking when moulting in late summer, and are surprisingly rarely seen for a few weeks. Then they emerge in fresh smart plumage, and singing ready for the approach of autumn. **Habitat** woods, gardens, parks. **Nest** in a cavity in a bank or a wall, in a thick bush or amongst ivy; or in an open nest-box. The 4–6 eggs hatch after 13–14 days and the young fly within two weeks. There may be two or three broods. **Food** largely insects, small worms, berries, scraps. **Voice** includes a sharp *tic tic* and a thin, elusive, but frequently heard high-pitched *sweeee*. The song is rich and musical, very expressive, especially in autumn when it seems more than usually wistful; short, liquid phrases run together in long, varied songs given often from a high perch, and sometimes at night especially near artificial lights.

Nightingale
Luscinia megarhynchos

Length: 16 cm
2

Weight: 20–25 g
S

Although so famous, this bird is scarcely known by most people; many so-called 'Nightingales' are in fact Robins which sing beside street lights at night! Real Nightingales are rarely found so close to habitation, preferring secluded thickets where their powerful song may dominate the dawn chorus. The song can also be heard during the day, but is perhaps at its best at dawn and dusk. The bird itself is neat, rather a bright rusty brown; its tail is more rufous, its under parts paler, and its head greyer, with a light ring round each eye. It is a little larger than a Robin or any of the warblers, but is usually very difficult to see well. Nightingales are found only in the southern half of England. **Habitat** coppiced woodland with thickets of hazel and chestnut, hawthorn brakes, bushes near heaths. **Nest** near the ground; 4–5 eggs laid in May hatch after 14 days and the young fly 11–12 days later. **Food** largely worms and insects taken from on or near the ground in overhung ditches or the floor of a wood. **Voice** several distinctive notes, especially a low, croaking *kerr* and a loud, sweet *weet* like a loud Chiffchaff's call. Song is loud, extremely rich and very rapid in parts; long *pew pew pew* notes, rising in pitch and ending in deep bubbling, are especially characteristic.

Redstart

Phoenicurus phoenicurus

Length: 13 cm

Weight: 12–18 g

2

S

Brightly coloured, but elusive, the Redstart may always be distinguished by its rusty-orange tail, though at rest the browner central feathers obscure some of the stronger colour. Males have blue-grey upper parts, with browner wings and an orange rump; the forehead makes a splash of white against the black face and throat. Females lack the head pattern and are much browner overall, with a soft shade of orange-buff underneath. The black eye stands out well. Males may be located by their song, often given from the top of a tall tree, but they are hard to spot amongst thick foliage. Redstarts often feed low down, however, and also take insects in the air, like flycatchers. **Habitat** deciduous woods and parks with old trees, especially oak; also bushy woodland edges on hillsides and rocky slopes with scattered trees. **Nest** in a hole or nest-box; six eggs are laid in May, which hatch after 12–14 days and the young fly in 14 days. **Food** largely insects; some berries in the autumn. **Voice** includes a *hooeet* (like the note of a Willow Warbler), and a liquid *twik*. Song is short but musical, starting with two or three low *srree srree* notes which turn into a bright, scratchy or rattling, abruptly ended warble.

Whinchat

Saxicola rubetra

Length: 13 cm

Weight: 17–20 g

2

S

Unlike the similar, and closely related, Stonechat, the Whinchat is purely a summer visitor. Males are easy to identify, as they have a nearly-black mask with a broad pale stripe above and below, and a pale chin. Females are duller and the young duller still, with the face pattern less obvious and closer to that of a young Stonechat, but always with a paler throat. Whinchats also have paler upper parts and white patches each side of the tail. In behaviour, they are restless birds, perching on top of stalks or bushes, and calling frequently. **Habitat** generally places similar to those favoured by Stonechats—rough ground, edges of meadows, young conifers—but often with the grass and herbs longer, and with more bushes. **Nest** on the ground, well-hidden in long grass. It lays 5–6 eggs, which hatch after 13 days. The young fly after 13 days in the nest. **Food** mainly insects. **Voice** similar to Stonechat's, but not so hard, with the *chat* note softer and the *wheet* or *tu* more musical and stronger. Song is variable, at best like a Robin's with chattering notes mixed in; often a less developed, chattering warble.

Stonechat

Saxicola torquata

Length: 13 cm

Weight: 14–17 g

R

A bold, noticeable little bird which sits on top of a bush or tall stem, or on a wire or some similarly exposed place, calling frequently, especially if disturbed near a nest with young. Stonechats are dumpy, but sit very upright, looking large-headed but short-tailed. They fly constantly from one perch to another, low over the ground; very often they are in pairs all the year round. The male has a black head and chin, with a white collar and a rusty breast; the hen is paler and browner, with just the suggestion of a similar head pattern. Unlike Whinchats, both have dark tails, and lack the Whinchat's pale stripe over the eye. **Habitat** gorsy commons and heaths, young plantations, bushy or brambly areas near the coast and rough grazing above sea cliffs. **Nest** on or near the ground. Lays 5–6 eggs in a well-hidden nest; they hatch after 14 days, and the young spend a further 12–13 days in the nest. **Food** mainly insects and spiders. **Voice** a hard *tsak tsak* or *chat chat*, a sad-sounding *wheet* and, often, a combination of the two—*wheet chat-chat*. Song, from a perch or in flight, is a varied, quick warble.

Wheatear
Oenanthe oenanthe

Length: 14 cm
2

Weight: 20–30 g
S

One of the earliest summer visitors, the male Wheatear in fresh plumage in March is an extremely smart bird. With a pure grey back, brown-black wings and clear buff under parts, set off by a black mask, he looks very neat, standing upright in a ploughed field or on a grassy bank. In flight the Wheatear is even more striking, all ages and both sexes having a pure white rump and sides to the tail, with a black T-shape formed by the tip and centre of the tail. Females are browner than males, without the black mask, and young birds have bright buffy edges to the wing feathers. The Wheatear can occur almost anywhere on migration, but is chiefly found in the north and west. **Habitat** upland areas with a mixture of close-cropped grass, screes and rocky outcrops. **Nest** in a hole in the ground, amongst rocks or beneath a stone. Lays six eggs which hatch after 14 days; the young fly after 15 days. **Food** chiefly ground insects, but it will also catch flies in the air. **Voice** includes a hard *chack* or *weet chack chack*, and a buzzing note from the young. Song, given from a perch or in a steeply rising song flight, is a varied warble mixed with chattering sounds.

Ring Ouzel
Turdus torquatus

Length: 24 cm
3

Weight: 90–120 g
S

Superficially like a Blackbird, the Ring Ouzel is actually quite distinct. It is a slimmer, wilder, shyer bird of wide open spaces, living mostly up in the hills of the north and west. It spends the winter in the Mediterranean area. Males are black with greyer wings, and across the chest is a broad band of white. Females are duller and browner, with a duller gorget. Ring Ouzels can be easy to find—they have a loud song and noisy calls—but they may also be extremely elusive. They are adept at slipping over the top of a hill out of sight, or keeping behind a rock. **Habitat** moorlands and rocky places, especially where gorse, bracken and odd rowans or hawthorns grow up through boulders in a gully; more rarely in peat hags and bushy places on moors. **Nest** in thick vegetation. Lays 4–5 eggs in April; they hatch after two weeks and the young fly two weeks later. **Food** mainly worms, insects, berries. **Voice** includes loud piping notes, a harsh *tac tac tac*; song is loud, in quality resembling that of a Mistle Thrush, but usually even less varied, often merely a few piping notes repeated.

Blackbird

Turdus merula

Length: 25 cm

Weight: 80–100 g

3

R

The cock Blackbird—jet black all over except for a pale ring round each eye and a golden-yellow bill—is easy to recognize. Only the shorter-tailed, gregarious, busy Starling can in any way be mistaken for it. Females and young Blackbirds are brown, with paler throats and mottled or spotted breasts, but they are always darker and less clearly marked than the Song Thrush. The Blackbird, hopping across a lawn, or flying up to a fence or post to land with raised and fanned tail, is a very familiar sight all over the British Isles. **Habitat** gardens, parks, woods, hedgerows, also more open areas. **Nest** in a bush or hedge. Lays 4–5 eggs, which hatch after two weeks; the young fly two weeks later. There may be two or three broods. **Food** fruit, berries, seeds, worms. **Voice** includes: a thin, tremulous *seei*, longer than the Song Thrush's call and less penetrating than the Redwing's; a loud, clattering alarm rattle; and a ringing *pink pink*. Song is loud and musical, but often fading into an insignificant ending. It is mellower than the Song Thrush's, the phrases longer and not repeated, and more fluty and varied than that of the Mistle Thrush.

Fieldfare

Turdus pilaris

Length: 25 cm

Weight: 80–130 g

3

W

Unlike the Song Thrush and Mistle Thrush, the Fieldfare is purely a winter visitor. It arrives in September or October, in flocks often mixed with Redwings. They descend on berries and strip the hedgerows as they progress westwards, then move onto open fields. Fieldfares can be recognized by the combination of grey head and rump, chestnut back and black tail. The under parts are buff and white, spotted black, becoming richer, almost orange, and more boldly blotched in the spring. Under the wing is a flash of white. **Habitat** open country and agricultural land, especially with tall trees and hedges where the flocks settle after being disturbed from the fields. **Food** varied: slugs, worms, insects, berries of all sorts. **Voice** very characteristic, a loud, harsh *chak ak ak* with a slight squeaky quality about it, but deep and raucous; in flight also a Lapwing-like *wee-eep*.

Song Thrush
Turdus philomelos

Length: 22 cm

3

Weight: 70–90 g

R

This is the familiar, common thrush of gardens, lawns and parks. It is smaller than a Blackbird, rather more dumpy and shorter-tailed, and *much* paler than spotted young and female Blackbirds. The back is uniform olive-brown, the underside a delicate shade of yellow-buff, whiter beneath, with slightly V-shaped, brown-black spots aligned in wavy streaks on the side of the breast and more evenly scattered elsewhere. The Mistle Thrush is a bigger, shyer bird. Song Thrushes hop steadily across short grass, pausing to look for worms with head to one side, before moving on again or wrestling with a big, juicy earthworm. **Habitat** gardens, parks, woods, overgrown hedges. **Nest** in a low bush or amongst ivy. Lays 4–5 blue eggs, black-spotted, in a mud-lined nest. They hatch after two weeks and the young fly two weeks later. **Food** largely worms and snails, which are smashed against a stone; also insects, berries. **Voice** includes a rattling alarm, and a distinctive thin *sip* or *sit*. The song is loud and far-carrying, extremely musical and varied, with each short phrase repeated two, three or more times. This repetition distinguishes the song from that of the Blackbird.

Redwing

Turdus iliacus

Length: 21 cm

2

Weight: 60–70 g

W

Like the Fieldfare, with which it is often to be found, the Redwing is a winter visitor.   Even smaller than a Song Thrush, the Redwing is easily distinguished by the cream stripe over the eye and another below the dark ear coverts, giving a head pattern bolder than that on any other thrush. At rest, the flanks show a rusty red patch, which is best seen extending to the red underwing in flight.   The upper parts are a rich, dark olive-brown; the underside silky white with streaks of dark spots forming lines more obvious than those of the Song Thrush.   Redwings are shy and quick to take flight, but become bolder in hard weather when, hungry and weak, they come to gardens and roadside verges and are easily approached.   **Habitat** farmland with hedges and trees; woods and thickets with blackberries and hawthorns.   **Food** largely berries and worms.   **Voice** long, thin *see* or *seep*, often given in flight. This note can frequently be heard overhead on clear autumn nights (but immigrant Song Thrushes sound much the same).   Also a rattling alarm note.

Mistle Thrush
Turdus viscivorus

Length: 26 cm
3
Weight: 110–140 g
R

Many people are surprised to find how large a Mistle Thrush looks. It is much bigger than a Song Thrush, with longer wings and tail. The overall effect is greyer, too, although the under parts are yellow-buff, with bigger, broader spots than those of the Song Thrush. The closed wings show pale feather edges which give a less uniform appearance, and in flight the whitish sides to the tail and large white areas under the wing are good points to notice. Young Mistle Thrushes cause a lot of confusion—they have white spots over the head, and broad scaly white marks over the upper parts. Mistle Thrushes leap along in bounding hops, then pause with head up and wings drooped. They are bold and aggressive near the nest. **Habitat** woods, copses, gardens, parks, bushy hillsides. **Nest** in a fork of a tree. Builds a large nest and lays four eggs in March or April. These hatch after two weeks and the young fly two weeks later. **Food** largely fruit and berries, also worms. **Voice** main call is a rattling or churring chatter. Song is loud, wild, throaty warbling, in short phrases with little variation.

Grasshopper Warbler
Locustella naevia

Length: 13 cm
2

Weight: 12–15 g
S

The *Locustella* warblers are all slim, elusive birds with rather long, rounded tails. This is the only one seen at all commonly in the British Isles; and it may be separated from Reed and Sedge Warblers by its almost mouse-like behaviour, the soft streaking on its olive upper parts, with little hint of rusty colouring and no stripe over the eye, and the pale buff or rather yellow under parts with a few thin streaks and dark smudges under the tail. With patience and careful stalking, a singing bird can be approached closely and seen in detail, when the subtly patterned feathering looks very attractive. **Habitat** rough grass, sedges, brambles and low bushes, sometimes plantations on moors. **Nest** on or near the ground. The six eggs are incubated for 13–15 days; the young fly after 10–12 days. **Food** insects and spiders. **Voice** very distinctive indeed. The song is a long, high-pitched reeling noise of even pace and pitch, sometimes continued for a minute or two without a break; it is a sharp, rattling, very rapid trill. Also a loud, sharp *tchik*.

Sedge Warbler

Acrocephalus schoenobaenus

Length: 13 cm
2

Weight: 10–13 g
S

A summer visitor, like the Reed Warbler, but less restricted to reeds, the Sedge Warbler can easily be distinguished by the broad band of cream over its eye. The back is softly streaked, but the rump is a pale sandy or tawny colour. Sedge Warblers are active, busy birds, often drawing attention to themselves with loud calls and song. The flight is low and flitting, usually for short distances only, and it may be difficult to get a good view as the bird descends into dense cover. **Habitat** reeds, osier beds, nettles and willowherb, with scattered bushes, brambles, etc. Usually in damp places. **Nest** in thick vegetation, near the ground. The 5–6 eggs hatch after two weeks' incubation, and the young fly two weeks later. **Food** largely insects, including aphids from reeds in autumn, taken to build up fat and energy for migration flights. **Voice** a scolding note, *tucc* or *chirr*. Song is more varied, less repetitive than that of the Reed Warbler, given from bushes or reeds or in a rising song flight. Quick and vigorous, often mimicking the song of other birds, it mixes bright whistles and pure notes with churrs and chattering sounds.

Reed Warbler
Acrocephalus scirpaceus

Length: 13 cm
2

Weight: 10–15 g
S

The Reed Warbler is generally quite unobtrusive as it slips quietly through the tall reeds which it prefers to inhabit. It is not found in Scotland or Ireland. Fortunately for birdwatchers, the males have a loud song and all have deep calls which attract attention. The bird is slender, brown and almost unmarked with any obvious pattern. Its under parts are buff, almost white on the throat; the soft brown upperside becomes almost rufous on the rump. Compared with the Garden Warbler and other plain warblers, it has a longer, rather rounded tail and a longer face and bill. **Habitat** mostly in reeds, beside lakes or rivers or in extensive marshes; also waterside willows and osiers and damp, reedy ditches. **Nest** in the reeds. It makes a grassy cup attached to reed stems, laying four eggs in June, which hatch after 11 days; the young fly after 11–12 days. Cuckoos often lay in the Reed Warbler's nest. **Food** largely insects caught around the edges of the marsh; also berries in autumn. **Voice** includes a low *churr*. Song is rather low, rambling, with each phrase repeated two or three times to give a distinctive rhythm of churring, squeaky and chirping notes, and lacking the Sedge Warbler's vehemence—*chrr chrr trik trik trik, chirup chirup*, etc.

Lesser Whitethroat
Sylvia curruca

Length: 13 cm
2

Weight: 10–15 g
S

A fraction smaller, neater and tidier-looking than a Whitethroat, the Lesser Whitethroat has duller, browner upper parts which lack the rusty colour so obvious on its relative. The male's darker grey head contrasts more with its white throat. This species also has dark legs, a feature helpful for identification. The tail is shorter, not so eye-catching as the slender, longer tail of the Whitethroat. **Habitat** similar to that of the Whitethroat, but it is less in low bushes, more in old, overgrown hedges and dense thickets. Not found in Scotland or Ireland. **Nest** in a hedge or bush. The 4–6 eggs hatch after 10–11 days, and the young fly after about another 10–11 days. **Food** largely insects and berries. **Voice** includes a hard *tak*, sharper than that of Blackcap or Garden Warbler, sometimes sounding more like *chik*; also a very thin, high squeak. The song is a more or less developed low even warble, suddenly changing to a rapid rattle on one note—*chikikikikik*. In the spring this hard, rattling note is often the best clue that a Lesser Whitethroat is concealed somewhere in a thick hedge. It has a most distinctive hollow, unmusical quality.

Whitethroat

Sylvia communis

Length: 14 cm

Weight: 14–18 g

2

S

Compared with the Blackcap, this is a lighter, slimmer, longer-tailed bird. It is also livelier and busier, restlessly flitting about in bushes and undergrowth and scolding intruders. Its slim tail is often raised and gives it a slightly untidy look in flight. The grey head of the male (brown for females and the immature) and, at all ages and in both sexes, the pure white throat, pinkish breast, brown back with rusty feather edgings on the wing, and white outer tail feathers, make it easy to recognize. Often a Whitethroat sits with crown feathers raised in a peak, giving a lively, perky effect. **Habitat** bushy places; rough ground with brambles, willowherb and nettles; hedges, woodland edges. **Nest** in low bushy growth. The 4–5 eggs hatch after 11–13 days, and the young leave the nest 10–12 days later. **Food** mainly insects, but berries in the autumn, sometimes currants, honeysuckle, etc, taken in gardens. **Voice** buzzy, churring notes often given from deep inside a bush—*charr, tak tak*, and a nasal *wheet wheet witwitwit*. Song is often given in a special rising display flight, with long wings whirring and flicking tail, but also from a perch; a lively, chattering warble of no great musical quality.

Garden Warbler
Sylvia borin

Length: 14 cm
2

Weight: 15–20 g
S

One of the plainest birds we have, the summer-visiting Garden Warbler is a soft, rather pale brown shade, paler beneath. Apart from a very slight pale mark from eye to bill and a subtle grey patch on the side of its neck, it is practically unmarked. A fresh-plumaged bird, with fine pale edges to its wing feathers and a large, bright eye, is, nevertheless, very attractive. It has a rather round head and a short, stout bill, which helps to distinguish it from other unmarked warblers; it is also relatively heavy in build. **Habitat** open woodland, bushy woodland edges, scattered trees, bushy commons. **Nest** in a bush or hedge. Lays 4–5 eggs, which hatch after 12 days; the young fly only 9–10 days later. **Food** largely insects, with more berries later in the summer and in autumn. **Voice** includes a hard *tak* like the Blackcap's, and a slightly softer 'chuffing' note. Song is sometimes barely distinguishable from that of some Blackcaps, but typically it is softer, more even and more prolonged—a rich warble, given from trees and bushes.

Blackcap

Sylvia atricapilla

Length: 14 cm

Weight: 15–20 g

2

S

Some Blackcaps winter in the British Isles, often visiting gardens and bird-tables, but most arrive here in April and leave by October. Males are greyish warblers, browner above, with little strong pattern except for a dull black cap. This is smaller, more 'peaked' and narrower above the bill than on the black-capped tits (which also have black chins). Females have a brown cap and young birds have more rufous ones. Blackcaps spend much of their time in bushy undergrowth in woods, but can sometimes more easily be seen in autumn, feeding from honeysuckle and elderberry bushes. **Habitat** open woodland with undergrowth, bushy places, gardens with trees. **Nest** in a bush or hedgerow; lays five eggs which hatch after 10–11 days. The young fly 10–13 days later. **Food** largely insects and berries. **Voice** includes a hard *tak*. This note, coming from a thicket or tree, is usually a sign of one of the *Sylvia* warblers. Song is rich and clear after a scratchy start, bursting into a rapid phrase of beautiful warbling notes—more of an outburst than the steadier, longer song of the Garden Warbler but subject to variation which can confuse the issue.

Wood Warbler
Phylloscopus sibilatrix

Length: 12 cm
2

Weight: 8–13 g
S

Compared with the very similar Willow Warbler, this is a rather larger bird. Its wings are distinctly longer and sometimes slightly drooped beside the tail. The upper parts are a clearer green, except for browner wings lined with yellow feather edges, providing a useful contrast with the uniform wings of the Willow. The Wood Warbler also has a broad dark line through the eye and a much more striking, pale yellow stripe above it; and the throat is yellow, above silky-white under parts. All these features give it a brighter, cleaner appearance than either Willow Warbler or Chiffchaff usually have. The Wood Warbler is widespread in the west and south of Britain, rare in the midlands and east, and absent in Ireland, and is very rarely seen on migration away from its breeding sites (whereas the other two turn up almost anywhere). **Habitat** tall woods especially of western sessile oak or beech, with little or no undergrowth. **Nest** on the ground amongst dead leaves on the open woodland floor. The 6–7 eggs laid in May hatch after 13 days. The young fly after 11–12 days. **Food** mainly insects. **Voice** a liquid *pew*, louder and less disyllabic than in the Chiffchaff or Willow Warbler. Two forms of song: one like a loud, clear repetition of the call note *pew pew pew*; the other quite different, starting with a stuttering series of short, sharp notes which speed up into a high, fast, shivering trill, *tip tip tititit't't'trrrrrrr*.

Chiffchaff

Phylloscopus collybita

Length: 10 cm
I

Weight: 7–9 g
S

Very much like the Willow Warbler, the Chiffchaff is best distinguished by its voice. However, it tends to be duller, less green; it has a rounder head, shorter wings and a slightly shorter tail. Its legs are always very dark, including the feet. It also tends to have a more markedly pale eye-ring. It is generally less common, and is absent from large areas in the north; a few over-winter, but most Chiffchaffs arrive in March and April (earlier than the Willow Warbler). Chiffchaffs are lively little birds, often flicking their wings as they feed amongst leaves. **Habitat** woods with thick undergrowth, but not conifers; bushy places with trees, requiring tall trees much more than does the Willow Warbler. **Nest** just above the ground; makes a ball-shaped nest with a side entrance. The 4–7 eggs are laid in May and hatch after 13 days; the young fly after 14 days. There may be two broods. **Food** mostly insects, some berries in autumn. **Voice** includes a sweet *hweet*, less disyllabic than from the Willow Warbler, but very similar. Song very distinct: a prolonged series of short, sharp notes repeated in irregular succession, *chip sip sap sap sip sap sew sit*, etc; or, simply *chiff chaff*, repeated at various pitches. Often interspersed with low, grating churrs.

Willow Warbler
Phylloscopus trochilus

Length: 10 cm
I

Weight: 8–10 g
S

A delicate, lightweight, greenish bird that flits about amongst foliage, picking minute insects from the leaves, is likely to be one of the *Phylloscopus* warblers. The Willow Warbler is present from April to September, and is common almost everywhere; spring adults are olive above and pale yellowish below, but soon become less green and fresh. Juveniles in late summer are greener, strongly yellow-tinged above, and pale, bright yellow beneath. The head pattern is fairly strong, with a dark eyestripe and a pale line above it, but otherwise the plumage rather lacks distinctive features. Note the brown legs with yellowish feet, and thin dark bill. The song is an excellent feature. **Habitat** woodland, mixed or deciduous, especially with a thick shrub layer; bushy places on heaths, commons, upland birchwoods, hedgerows. **Nests** on the ground amongst thick grass. The 6–7 eggs are laid in May, incubated for 13 days and the young fly after 14 days. **Food** chiefly insects. **Voice** includes a distinctive, sweet *hooeet*, more disyllabic than in the Chiffchaff. The song is sweet and liquid, a clear series of notes gaining volume and then fading away again, without the variation and rattling quality of Chaffinch song and stronger than the Treecreeper's; no other song really resembles it.

Goldcrest
Regulus regulus

Length: 9 cm
I

Weight: 5–7 g
R

Barely half the weight of the Wren, this is our tiniest bird. It is rather like a small but somewhat dumpy warbler, or a small kind of tit. The minute size, call and song all help to distinguish it; but as it is often seen high in dense conifer foliage, it does not show its plumage features well. A closer view reveals a generally green appearance, brighter above and paler below, with dark and light bars across the wing (unmarked in warblers), a pale face with a smudgy 'moustache' and dark eye, and a dark crown stripe with a thin yellow central line. Goldcrests are often in small groups or mixed with Blue and Coal Tits, and roam through the woods at random outside the breeding season. **Habitat** mixed and coniferous woods, and parks with ornamental conifers; more widespread in winter. **Nest** near the end of a horizontal, spreading branch; it makes a tiny, mossy nest slung beneath the foliage. The 7–10 eggs hatch after two weeks and the young fly after about three weeks. There are two broods. **Food** spiders and insects. **Voice** a thin, high shrill *zeec zeec zeec*, much as given by several of the tits, but more colourful than in the Long-tailed Tit and more penetrating than from the others. Song is high, thin, quick and rhythmic—*tidlde-ee* rapidly repeated several times before a flourish at the end.

Spotted Flycatcher
Muscicapa striata

Length: 14 cm
2

Weight: 14–18 g
S

Dull and inconspicuous, the Spotted Flycatcher is nevertheless full of character, and fascinating to watch. Its flycatching sallies are its most notable feature. From a perch in trees bordering a woodland clearing, from a big evergreen on a lawn's edge, or from a fence, stump, gravestone or park bench, it suddenly flies out to twist and turn after a passing insect. On their lookout posts, Spotted Flycatchers sit upright, appearing slim and long in wing and tail, with a large-eyed look of concentration and alertness. They are pale brown above, with light feather edgings on the wings, and are lighter, but not quite white, underneath. The forehead and chest have soft, darker streakings. **Habitat** parks, large gardens, tennis courts, woods and woodland edges, often near buildings. **Nest** in ivy, creepers on walls, or in the old nest of another bird. The 4–5 eggs are laid in late May or early June— the flycatcher is a summer visitor which arrives late—and hatch after 14 days. The young fly after 12–13 days. **Food** almost entirely insects caught on the wing; some taken from the ground, but not picked from foliage like the warblers' prey. **Voice** includes a thin, high *tzee*, and a *tzee-tzuc*. Song is infrequent and nondescript.

Pied Flycatcher
Muscicapa hypoleuca

Length: 13 cm
2

Weight: 10–15 g
S

This bird is much less familiar than the Spotted Flycatcher, being largely restricted to the west of Britain except as an autumn (less often as a spring) migrant which may appear on our coasts and occasionally inland. The male in summer is black above, white below, with a large white wing patch, white outer tail feathers and white forehead spots. The female and young birds are brown and dull white but with a similar pattern, except that the white wing markings are narrower. They look a little like small, slender female Chaffinches but without an upper wing-bar. Pied Flycatchers take insects on the ground more than do the Spotted, and feed more often in open spaces within woods. Despite their conspicuous pattern, they are remarkably elusive in the dappled sun and shade of a wood. **Habitat** oak woods in hilly country, wooded valleys, lines of oak and alder along upland streams. **Nest** in a nest-box or natural tree hole. The 5–9 eggs are laid late in May and hatch after 12–13 days. The young fly when two weeks old. **Food** mostly insects. **Voice** includes a sharp *whit*, *tic* and *h'weet*. Song is quite musical, with a rather faltering effect instead of a flowing warble, the notes tending to be separated before the final flourish—*see sip see beebidi bidi*, or similar phrases.

Bearded Tit
Panurus biarmicus

Length: 17 cm
2

Weight: 13–20 g
R

Though this bird is not really a tit, attempts to bring into general use the better name Bearded Reedling have always failed. But the word 'reedling' well describes both its small size and its habitat; the bird is restricted to extensive reed-beds, which, unfortunately, have become increasingly rare, now almost entirely in the east and south of England. In flight low over the reeds, with whirring wings and a long, trailing tail, it looks almost like a tiny pheasant! Males have blue heads with a broad, black moustache; females and young have no blue-grey, but tawny heads without moustaches. They are all bright tawny on the body, variably striped with buff and black according to age and sex. After the breeding season, families join in large bands which roam the reed-beds, hard to see on a dull or windy day but always identifiable by their calls. **Habitat** reeds. **Nest** in reeds. Lays 5–7 eggs, which hatch after 12–13 days; the young fly 9–12 days later. There may be two or three broods. **Food** largely seeds of reed, taken from the seed-heads or from the litter on the ground beneath. **Voice** loud and ringing, with a bell-like *ping* or *chink*.

Long-tailed Tit
Aegithalos caudatus

Length: 14 cm
2

Weight: 8–9 g
R

Barely as heavy as a Wren, this tiny bird is more than half tail. Often in small flocks or family parties of a dozen or so, Long-tailed Tits travel through hedgerows and bushy places, keeping contact by thin calls, and drifting a few at a time from bush to bush. They rarely visit gardens and bird-tables, but will mix with other tits in autumn and winter flocks. The silhouette alone is enough for identification, but it may be confirmed by a view of the pink, black and white plumage. (White-headed race on left is rare.) Young birds lack pink. **Habitat** bushy edges of woods, scrub, thickets, overgrown hedges, cuttings, quarries, etc. **Nest** in a thick, often thorny bush, sometimes high in a tree. The nest is a rounded mass of moss, lichens and cobwebs, lined with feathers, with a side entrance. Eight or more eggs are laid in April, hatching after 14–18 days. The young fly after 15–16 days of being cramped in the nest, already with long tails. **Food** insects, seeds, buds. **Voice** is a good indication of their presence—a thin, high, but rather featureless and unmusical *zee-zee-zee*, and a deep, abrupt, rolled *trrp*.

Marsh Tit
Parus palustris

Length: 12 cm
I

Weight: 10–12 g
R

A brown-and-buff tit, with glossy black cap and small black chin patch, this bird is extremely similar to the Willow Tit; it lacks the wing-bars and white nape spot of the Coal Tit. Compared with a Willow Tit it tends to be sleeker, greyer, and more uniform. It fortunately has one very distinct call. It is rare in gardens, and its patchy distribution leaves it far less familiar than the commoner tits. It does not occur in Scotland or Ireland. **Habitat** woods, especially open woods of oak and other deciduous trees; more rarely hedges, gardens and thickets. **Nest** in a natural hole in a tree. It lays 7–8 eggs in April or May, which hatch after 13 days; the young fly after 16–17 days. **Food** chiefly insects, but also berries, beech-mast. **Voice** is important in identification. It is worth learning all calls heard from the black-capped tits. If the bird calls a bright, whistling *pitchoo* or *p'tew*, it is a Marsh Tit. Also gives a thin *see see see*, and a buzzy, nasal *chika deedeedee*. Song is a repetition of a slightly flat note in a bubbling trill: *scipipipipipip*.

Willow Tit
Parus montanus

Length: 12 cm
I

Weight: 9–11 g
R

Extremely like the Marsh Tit, the Willow looks a little less neat and tidy. It is more bull-necked, with a bigger and less sharp chin patch, a longer and looser looking black cap extending down the nape, rather white cheeks and, in fresh plumage, a less greyish back and more rusty or orange-buff sides to its body. All these features are subtle and variable. On the closed wing pale edges to the secondary feathers make a more or less conspicuous light panel or streak, often a useful clue. Use the voice for identification if you can. **Habitat** much like that of the Marsh Tit, but also damper sites which the Marsh Tit avoids, despite its name. Also thickets and tall, old hedges. **Nest** in a hole in a soft, rotten stump, excavated by the birds themselves. Lays 8–9 eggs which hatch after 14 days; the young fly after about 17–19 days. **Food** includes insects and spiders; also nuts and berries. **Voice** lacks anything like the Marsh Tit's *pitchoo* note—if the bird gives that call it is not a Willow Tit! Has thin *see see see* and similar calls, but most useful for identification is a deep, nasal, buzzing *zair zair zair*. Song is usually a liquid, pure whistle repeated several times, rather like that of a Wood Warbler, but quicker and less even—*pew pew pew* or *syu syu syu*.

Coal Tit
Parus ater

Length: 11 cm
I

Weight: 8–10 g
R

Even smaller than the Blue Tit, the Coal Tit is easily distinguished from the other tits by the patch of white on the back of its head, surrounded in black. It is dull brownish above and buff below, with no blue, green or yellow, but has white bars across its wings and a large black throat patch. It does visit gardens, but in most areas is much less frequent at the peanut bag than Blue or Great Tits. The Coal Tit has a tendency to keep higher, in thicker foliage, than the others and more patience may be needed to get a good view of it. **Habitat** woods, parks and gardens, often with a preference for conifers. **Nest** in holes in trees close to the ground, or in a crevice in a stump or wall, or in the ground itself. The 7–11 eggs are laid in April or May, and hatch after 17–18 days. The young fly after 16 days. There is only one brood each year. **Food** mainly insects and spiders; also seeds, nuts, fat. **Voice** includes thin, high-pitched *see see* notes, a louder, richer *tsew* and a two-note song resembling a sweeter, less strident version of the Great Tit's—*teechu teechu teechu*.

Blue Tit
Parus caeruleus

Length: 12 cm
I

Weight: 9–14 g
R

Everyone's favourite, the Blue Tit is easy to distinguish from all the other birds at a bird-table by its blue cap, wings and tail, and its yellow under parts, marked only with a thin dark streak on its belly. In the woods in late summer and on through the winter, mixed flocks of tits roam in search of food. The Blue Tit keeps more to the thinner, outer twigs than the heavyweight Great Tit, its acrobatic abilities allowing it to reach for seeds or look for spiders on the most slender shoots. In spring the parties break up and pairs establish territories. Blue Tits may then be seen in gliding, butterfly-like flights from tree to tree, advertising their presence and 'ownership' of their little patch. **Habitat** woods, thick hedges, gardens, parks, orchards; in winter also reed-beds, overgrown ditches, scrubby areas. **Nest** in a natural or artificial hole. It lays 7–14 eggs in April or May. The young hatch after 14 days and fly after 19 days in the nest. **Food** insects and spiders, grain, seeds and buds. **Voice** includes thin *tsee see see, tsee si-si-sit* and variants. Song is less strident than the Great Tit's, running into a rapid trill: *tsee tsee si tsuhuhuhuhuhu.*

Great Tit

Parus major

Length: 14 cm

Weight: 16–21 g

2

R

Bold and aggressive, the Great Tit is a familiar bird at garden feeding posts. Its acrobatic feeding techniques—whether on peanut bags, baskets of scraps or on thin twigs in search of seeds—combine with a striking pattern of black, white, green, yellow and blue to make it universally popular. The black top to its head, bold white cheeks and black stripe down its front make it easily recognizable. Great Tits spend more time on the ground than Blue Tits, and tend to feed lower and on larger branches and twigs than the smaller tits which can risk the more spindly perches. **Habitat** woods, mostly deciduous, gardens, orchards. **Nest** in a natural hole or in a box. Lays 5–11 eggs in April or May, which hatch after 14 days; the young fly after 18–20 days. There is only one brood, timed to arrive when the number of caterpillars is greatest. **Food** includes insects and spiders, seeds, nuts, buds. **Voice** very varied (very often a strange noise will turn out to emanate from a Great Tit), including a thin *tsee tsee tsee*, a ringing *tink tink tink* and scolding churrs. Song is a metallic double note, repeated endlessly—*teechu-teechu-teechu*.

Nuthatch
Sitta europaea

Length: 14 cm
2

Weight: 20–24 g
R

This stocky, rather stiff little bird is very distinctive in its soft blue-grey, buff and rusty plumage, set off by a streak of black through the eye.   It has short, but strong legs, with sharp claws enabling it to grip even smooth bark tightly enough to cling to any branch, at any angle.   Unlike the woodpeckers, it is quite at ease coming down head first! Its calls, especially in spring, best help us to locate it.   Late in the summer, when they are quiet, Nuthatches can be very difficult to see high up in the dense foliage of a beech tree.   Where gardens are near to a wood or park, Nuthatches may come to the bird-table or nut bag. **Habitat** woods and well-wooded parks, usually with mature deciduous trees.   Not found in northern Britain or in Ireland.   **Nest** in a hole or nest-box, plastering the entrance with mud until the hole is just the right size. Six or more eggs are laid in April or May; they hatch after 14 days and the young fly after 23–25 days.   **Food** includes beech-mast, acorns, seeds, insects and hazelnuts. **Voice** loud and far-carrying.   A metallic, lively *chwit chwit*, often repeated; a piping *twee*; and a rapid, trilling whistle.

Treecreeper
Certhia familiaris

Length: 13 cm
2

Weight: 8–11 g
R

Although primarily a woodland bird, the Treecreeper is less restricted to mature trees than the Nuthatch. However, while the Nuthatch often feeds on the ground, the Treecreeper never does; it must always live close to the tree-trunk, searching the bark for food as it climbs upwards. It may spiral around a trunk, or cling beneath a branch, before moving on to the bottom of the next tree and starting again. It moves in a jerky shuffle, pressed against the tree but showing its white under parts from the side. Above, it is a rich, rather rusty brown, marked with buff and white. A long pale bar shows on the wing in flight. **Habitat** woodland, strips of trees along riversides, tall old hedges. **Nest** in a crevice behind loose bark. It lays 3–8 eggs, which hatch after 17–20 days. The young fly after 14 days. **Food** chiefly insects and spiders. **Voice** includes a high, thin *seeee*. Song is not well-known, but in fact quite frequent and very distinctive—a sweet phrase of quick, high notes, descending before a flourish at the end: *tsip tseetseetsee-sip-ip-siweetit*.

Jay

Garrulus glandarius

Length: 34 cm

Weight: 160 g

4

R

If a Jay is bold enough to come to a lawn early one morning, or confident of protection in a park, it may give a good enough view for its beautiful colours and pattern to be fully appreciated. The striped crest, black moustache, black and white wings with a streak of rust and a vivid blue patch, black tail and white rump all contrast strongly with the soft pink of the body plumage. Normally, however, it tends to disappear, with a characteristic screech, giving just a glimpse of the big white patch over its tail. Although largely insectivorous or vegetarian, the Jay is unnecessarily persecuted everywhere and generally very shy, which is a great pity. **Habitat** woods, thick hedgerows, parks and wooded gardens. **Nest** in shrubbery or low on the side-shoots of a tree. The 5–6 eggs laid in May hatch after 16 days; the young fly after three weeks. **Food** chiefly berries, seeds and, especially, acorns which are buried in the autumn and eaten during the winter and following spring. Also beetles, small animals, birds and eggs. **Voice** includes a mewing note and, most distinctive, a loud, harsh, sudden shriek, like the tearing of stiff cloth—*skaak*.

Magpie

Pica pica

Length: 45 cm

Weight: 240 g

4

R

Half the length of the Magpie is tail. Combined with its pied plumage, this long, slender shape makes it an unmistakable bird. Its feeding habits are the subject of controversy, but it is, in fact, very largely insectivorous. Magpies take some eggs and young birds, but far fewer than do cats (or Sparrowhawks), and their persecution is often unjustified. Showing green, purple and blue gloss, they are beautiful birds at close quarters, and their social behaviour is fascinating. Where they are common, large flocks form late in the winter and in spring, but Magpies are perhaps most often seen in pairs. **Habitat** farmland with thick, tall hedges and trees; less often in more open or more wooded country. In some places they visit gardens. **Nest** in a tall tree or thicket, making a roofed nest of sticks (often conspicuous in the winter). The 5–8 eggs laid in April hatch after 17–18 days; the young, shorter-tailed than their parents, fly three weeks later. **Food** varied, includes insects, dead animals and birds, worms, grain, berries. **Voice** is harsh and chattering, *chatchatchatchatchak.*

Jackdaw
Corvus monedula

Length: 33 cm
4

Weight: 250 g
R

Jackdaws are curiously patchy in their distribution, but widespread and fairly common. They are smaller than other black crows, more the size of a pigeon. They have a neater, rounder shape, too, with more rounded wings. Unlike any other crow, the Jackdaw has a jet black cap contrasting with a greyer neck. The pale eye also confirms identification. Jackdaws are lively and gregarious, often joining Rooks to feed and fly to roost in large mixed flocks. **Habitat** woods and parks, with old trees providing nest sites; also church towers, old buildings, quarries and cliffs both inland and on the coast. **Nest** in a hole in a tree, building or cliff. The 4–6 eggs, laid in April or May, hatch after 17–18 days. The young leave the nest after 30–35 days. **Food** largely insects, small mammals, snails, frogs, worms and vegetable matter. **Voice** is distinctive, usually a sharp, fairly high-pitched *tchak* or *kyow*.

Rook
Corvus frugilegus

Length: 45 cm
4

Weight: 490 g
R

Rooks are splendid birds in their black plumage with blue and purple sheen and bare, grey face. They circle above the treetop colony, creating a comfortable, pleasing chorus of caws and croaks, or settle on the fields in scores, even hundreds, to march about in search of food. They seem to be a perfect part of the British scene. Compared with crows, they stand more upright but have more ragged plumage, and in particular have a steeper forehead, higher crown and a slimmer bill. In flight, the longer, rounder tail gives more possibility of confusion with a Raven. **Habitat** agricultural country with trees for nesting and roosting. Often in villages or the outskirts of towns. Sometimes moors, heaths, coastal flats. **Nest** in tall trees, in groups of a handful to hundreds of pairs. The big stick nest holds 3–5 eggs from March or April. These hatch after 16–18 days and the young fly after 29–30 days. **Food** largely vegetable, including grain, root crops and berries; but also insects, worms, small mammals. **Voice** usually *caw* or *kaah* and a more musical, slightly ⁻inging note; also a deeper, abrupt note close to the tone of a Raven's calls.

Carrion Crow

Corvus corone

Length: 46 cm

Weight: 570 g

4

R

The familiar black Carrion Crow of England and Wales is replaced in Ireland, the Isle of Man, and in much of Scotland by the grey and black **Hooded Crow**. They are both the same species, simply showing strong racial characteristics in plumage pattern. The Hooded Crow is unmistakable, showing much more grey than a Jackdaw, but the Carrion Crow is much closer to a Rook or Raven. The Raven, however, is bigger, with a longer head and tail, while the Rook has slightly rounder wings and a more rounded tail than the Crow, and adult Rooks have a bare face. Young Rooks do have black faces, but are more upright, with more ragged under parts (especially baggy thighs, like the adults) and slimmer bills than the sleeker-looking Carrion Crow. **Habitat** all kinds of open country: farmland, moors, coastal marshes, mudflats. **Nest** in isolation, in a tree (or a bush in hilly areas). Lays 4–5 eggs from early April. These hatch after 18–21 days, and the young fly after 4–5 weeks. **Food** includes small birds and mammals, alive or dead, eggs, grain, worms, beetles and all sorts of scraps washed up on the beach or on rubbish tips. **Voice** a deep, croaking *kraah*, often repeated, and less pleasing than the *caw* of a Rook.

Raven

Corvus corax

Length: 63 cm

Weight: 1–1·4 kg

5

R

In the wilder places of the country, a loud, echoing call may draw attention to a large, angular, black shape—the Raven. Although much bigger than a Crow, its size may not be obvious at a distance; but its powerful wingbeats, greater length of wing and tail and large protruding head give it a distinctive appearance. Overhead, it shows a wedge- or diamond-shaped tail (that of the Crow is square, but the Rook has a rather more similar tail shape). Its throat is ragged, almost bearded, and the feathers of the upper head and neck can be raised to give a grotesquely large-headed shape. The Raven also has a long, arched bill, suited for tearing at dead meat. Unlike the Crow, it is capable of prolonged soaring and Ravens may gather into aerobatic parties, diving and chasing. **Habitat** mountainous areas, moors, cliffs from sea-level to highland regions; locally over built-up areas. **Nest** in the top of a tall tree; more often on a crag, usually beneath an overhang. Four or more eggs, laid in February or March, hatch after three weeks; the young fly 5–6 weeks later. **Food** very varied: dead animals of all sorts, small live mammals and birds, insects, seeds. **Voice** is a distinctive aid to identification. The usual note is a deep, croaking *pruk pruk* or *crronk*; also a ringing, deep *tonk*.

Starling
Sturnus vulgaris

Length: 21 cm

3

Weight: 75–90 g

R

Crowds of Starlings, jostling and chattering together in a field, then suddenly taking flight to swirl around together or move to the next pasture, are characteristic of autumn and winter in the countryside. Great roosting flocks also settle in some big cities; and Starlings are almost always seen in every garden. The winter plumage (illustrated), heavily spotted with white and streaked with orange-brown on the wings, is unique. In summer they are less spotted, showing bright sheens of green and purple; the orange legs and yellow bill are distinctive. The triangular wings and short tail, upright stance, and quick shuffling run distinguish a Starling from a Blackbird even in silhouette. **Habitat** woodland, hedges, farmland with old trees, parks, gardens. **Nest** in a cavity in a tree or building. The 5–7 eggs laid from April onwards hatch in only 12–13 days and the young fly after three weeks; they look plain brown for a time. **Food** largely insects, spiders, wood-lice, etc, with more grain, seeds, berries in autumn and winter. **Voice** a loud, grating *tcheer*, clicks and whistles. Song, given from a perch with waving wings, is a long, rambling mixture of creaky whistles, trills and rattling noises.

House Sparrow
Passer domesticus

Length: 14 cm
2

Weight: 25–30 g
R

Seen in a garden, city or park, the House Sparrow seems hardly to need description. But odd birds in the countryside, especially in the drab plumage of autumn, cause more misidentifications than might be imagined. The male always has a grey top to the head, with a band of red-brown each side, and at least a small patch of black on the chin. His broad grey rump may also be very obvious, below the streaky back. Females and young have sandy-brown heads with a broad pale band above and behind the eye. Underneath all are grey-buff, with no streaks, whereas most finches and buntings have streaky markings. **Habitat** farmland, farmsteads, suburban and village gardens, town parks. **Nest** in a hole or cavity in a building, in dense creepers on walls, in tall hedges and ivy. The nest is large and untidy. Up to five eggs are usually laid, and hatch after 14 days; the young fly after 15 days. There may be three broods. **Food** largely grain, seeds, buds, insects, bread. **Voice** a mixture of cheeps and chirps, especially *cheeip* and *chrup*; this may develop into a kind of song.

Tree Sparrow
Passer montanus

Length: 13 cm
2

Weight 20–25 g
R

Many people overlook the Tree Sparrow, or think they know it when they don't, which is a pity. It is a small, neat and smart bird, often paler and sandier looking than the House Sparrow. It lacks the deep chestnut-brown of the House Sparrow's head bands but has, instead, a round cap of rich chocolate-brown. The Tree does not have the grey crown of a cock House Sparrow. It has whiter cheeks, with a large, square patch of black on each; a neater black bib, and stout black bill. Its rump is buffish, not grey. Males, females and young all look much alike. It is generally much less familiar to us than a House Sparrow, since it does not come into small gardens. **Habitat** deciduous woods with clearings; parks with old trees; some large gardens and orchards. Nests in a hole in a tree (or wall) or in a nest-box. Lays 4–6 eggs, which are incubated for 12–14 days; the young fly within two weeks. Two broods. **Food** largely seeds, etc; some insects. **Voice** includes chirrupings much like the House Sparrow's, but generally more musical. More useful for identification is the distinctive flight call—a hard, loud and abrupt *tek tek*.

Chaffinch

Fringilla coelebs

Length: 15 cm

Weight: 19–23 g

R

One of the commonest and most widespread birds, the Chaffinch is also easy to identify. On each wing is a broad band of white near the bend, and a thinner white bar across the greater coverts; also the outer tail feathers are mostly white. In flight, or getting up from the ground, it therefore shows a lot of flickering patches of pure white. Males have a blue-grey head with a dark mask in summer (duller in winter), a dark brown back, green rump and deep pinkish under parts (not nearly so red as those of a Bullfinch). Females are greyer overall, with a soft olive shade above and a subtle grey-pink colour beneath. Chaffinches are often in small, loose parties (for example, around lay-bys and picnic sites searching for scraps); in winter they join up in large flocks. **Habitat** woods, gardens, hedges; open ground and fields in winter. **Nest** in a bush, or low in a tree; the 4–5 eggs are incubated for 11–13 days. The young fly 14 days later. **Food** largely seeds, grain, berries; also insects, worms. **Voice** includes a number of calls: a loud, metallic *chink chink*, not unlike that of a Great Tit, is most frequent; a loud *hweet*; and a soft *tsup* in flight. Song is loud and bright, with a rattling quality, ending in a flourish: *chip chip chip tel tel tel chery-ery-ery tissi cheweeoo.*

Brambling

Fringilla montifringilla

Length: 15 cm

Weight: 22–30 g

2

W

As the scientific name shows, this bird is more closely related to the Chaffinch than is any other finch, and it is very similar in size, shape and actions. But it is only here in winter, when it may frequently be seen mixed with flocks of Chaffinches and Sparrows. The male has a bright orange-yellow patch across the wing as well as a thinner white bar, white in the tail and a narrow white rump. Underneath he is orange across the chest, with a silky-white belly. In winter the head is dark and smudgy, but by spring it becomes largely black. Females are paler and duller, with more yellow-buff about them and browner heads, but they also have the wing-bars and white rump. Bramblings are fond of beechwoods and, like Chaffinches, shuffle about quietly and unobtrusively on the ground, flying up steeply into the trees if disturbed. **Habitat** woods, hedgerows, stubble and ploughed fields; not a garden visitor. **Food** largely seeds, beech-mast, berries. **Voice** in flight is much like that of Chaffinch, but the *tsup* note is firmer and may be repeated more quickly; and there is a vulgar-sounding, nasal twang—*swairk* or *swank*.

Greenfinch
Carduelis chloris

Length: 14 cm
2

Weight: 25–30 g
R

Having taken advantage
of our increased habit of
feeding birds in gardens,
the Greenfinch is now a
familiar bird, often re-
garded as a greedy visitor to the bird-table. The males,
apple-green with grey wings striped with yellow and
yellow patches in the tail, are easy to identify. A dark
mask between the eye and the big, pale bill give them a
slightly angry look. Females are duller and often
browner, with less yellow in the wing, and young birds
are browner still, more sparrow-like, but all have some
yellow as a stripe along the edge of the closed wing, instead
of the pale bars across the wing of a sparrow. They are
bigger, plainer birds than Siskins. **Habitat** overgrown
hedges, thickets, wooded gardens, woodland clearings; in
winter, farmland and open ground near the sea. **Nest** in
a thick bush or hedge; the 4–6 eggs hatch in 13 days and
the young leave the nest when about two weeks old.
Food mainly seeds, berries, buds. **Voice** a rapid, jing-
ling twitter, *chichichichichi*, less rattling than a Redpoll's
but more even than a Linnet's. Also a squeaky *tsooee* and
in spring a deep, nasal *dzzwee*. The song, based on the
calls, is often given in a display flight, with wings fully
spread and flickering.

Goldfinch
Carduelis carduelis

Length: 12 cm
2

Weight: 14–17 g
R

This small slender finch
is so boldly coloured as to
be unmistakeable in a
good view. The black-
white-and-red face and
black and yellow wings make it a real gem. In flight,
even if the wings are not well seen, the black-and-white
tail and white rump show up well. Young birds in
autumn (lower illustration) are duller, with pale grey
heads; but they still have black wings with a broad band
of yellow. The Goldfinch needs tall plants with plenty of
seeds, such as thistles, sow-thistles and the yellow
dandelion-like composites. Where such plants abound,
either in the wild or where weeds are uncleared, flocks of
a score or two may gather, dancing around in light, bouncy
flight from one clump to the next. **Habitat** weedy fields,
waste places, overgrown building sites, parks, wood edges;
leafy trees in avenues and suburban areas; gardens.
Nest out on the swaying branch of a tree such as a
chestnut or cherry, or in an orchard. The 5–6 eggs hatch
in 12–13 days and the young fly 14 days later. **Food**
largely seeds, those of thistle, teazel, etc. **Voice** a sweet,
rippling twitter with a liquid quality: *tswit witwit witwit*.
Also louder, rasping notes. Song based on the twittering
call with more elaborate phrases, often given from high in
a tree.

179

Siskin
Carduelis spinus

Length: 12 cm
I

Weight: 12–17 g
R/W

One of our smallest and most attractive finches, the Siskin is known in most parts as a winter visitor. Small numbers do breed in the north and west but elsewhere they come to woods and belts of riverside trees in winter. In spring, when natural foods are scarce, increasing numbers visit peanut bags in gardens. Males are streaked green above, with a black cap and chin patch; beneath, they are vivid yellow-green. Females are paler, duller and more streaky, but they never look brown and, like the males, have flashes of yellow each side of the tail. Siskins are gregarious birds and flocks seem to rush from one place to another in energetic bursts, pouring out of one tree and disappearing just as suddenly into the next. **Habitat** woods of pine, spruce and larch; in winter alders, birches, damp copses. **Nest** on a high conifer branch tip. Lays 3–5 eggs in a tiny nest. Incubation is only 11–12 days, and the young fly after 15 days. **Food** largely seeds of trees; in autumn also of composites and various weeds. **Voice** a loud, clear, but slightly squeaky *tsy-ew, tsu-wee,* or *tsyzing,* often given in flight; also a loud, rapid chatter from flocks and a quiet, purring buzz from feeding birds. Song is not unlike that of Goldfinch, with the clear, ringing calls mixed in.

Linnet
Carduelis cannabina

Length: 14 cm
2

Weight: 14–20 g
R

This is a small brown finch (always more rufous or chestnut than the more heavily streaked Redpoll), with more or less contrast between the chestnut back and greyer head. Males have cleaner colours and less streaking than the females. All have dark wings and tail, with thin white feather edges which make pale panels. Spring males also have a rich red-pink chest and redder cap. Linnets form large flocks in the autumn (less commonly seen in winter) and even breed in loose colonies, so often several can be seen together. **Habitat** rough, bushy or gorsy places, with scattered bushes and grassy clearings; young plantations. **Nest** in a bush or hedge; 4–6 eggs hatch after 10–12 days, and the young fly 11–12 days later. **Food** mainly seeds of weeds and grasses, especially thistles, dandelions, mugwort, etc. **Voice** includes a rapid twitter, *chichichichit*, which lacks the ringing quality of a Greenfinch's call or the metallic sound of a Redpoll's, and is more uneven than either. Song is musical and varied, of a basic twittering character but with rich warbles included; groups may give a twittering version, more or less developed from the flight note.

Redpoll
Carduelis flammea

Length: 12 cm
I

Weight: 10–12 g
R

A tiny finch, always looking streaky brown with
pale buff bars across the
wing, the Redpoll is
fairly easy to tell if seen
well. Groups of small finches bounding along in flight
from tree to tree are most likely to be Redpolls or Siskins,
and then the voice should sort them out. All but very
young Redpolls have a little black chin patch and a deep
red forehead patch. Males in spring have a bright pink
or crimson flush on the breast. Although they will join
flocks of other finches in weedy fields, Redpolls are largely
birds of the trees, where they feed in an acrobatic way
almost like tits. **Habitat** woodland edges with birch
scrub, hawthorns, bushy commons, young plantations;
increasingly, bushy suburban gardens. **Nest** in a bush
or hedge. Lays 4–5 eggs in May or June; these hatch
after 10–11 days and the young fly within two weeks.
Food largely seeds of trees such as birch and alder, and
all kinds of weedy growth; also a few insects. **Voice** includes a loud, twangy *tsooee* and a most distinctive hard,
metallic, even *chuchuchuch*. Song includes this note
interspersed with a high, reeling trill, often given in flight.

Bullfinch
Pyrrhula pyrrhula

Length: 14 cm
2

Weight: 20–25 g
R

The male Bullfinch is one of the most attractive birds of our countryside, bright but not garish, subtle but not dull. It has a black cap and chin, blue-black wings and tail, with a band of grey and just a mark of pink on each wing; the back is pale blue-grey and the rump pure white. Beneath, the male is bright rich pink. Females are similar in pattern but much more subdued, the back browner, the under parts duller and less red. Young birds are like browner females with no black cap—but at all ages the big white rump patch shows well as the bird flies off through a hedge or disappears into a bush. **Habitat** hedges, thickets, shrubberies, bushy gardens, woodland with much undergrowth. **Nest** in a thick hedge or tall bush. It lays 4–5 eggs in May, which hatch after 12–14 days; the young leave the nest after 12–16 days. **Food** largely seeds, berries and buds; the young are fed on caterpillars. **Voice** includes a characteristic call note—a low, piping or fluty *pyoo* or *piew*. Song is infrequent and poorly developed, mostly a peculiar creaky piping sound.

Snow Bunting
Plectrophenax nivalis

Length: 17 cm

2

Weight: 30–35 g

W

Although a few breed in northern hills, this is predominantly a winter visitor to a few high areas inland and to the east coast. Odd birds may turn up from time to time by reservoirs inland. On the coast in winter small flocks feed on the beach or on a nearby marsh, flying up when disturbed to move rapidly away a few hundred metres, or to swing round and return almost to the same spot. As they settle, the birds seem to melt away and disappear as quickly as they came. On the ground they shuffle along on short legs, but they are long, stout buntings. Males show much white, but have smudgy red-brown marks on the crown, cheeks and sides of the chest. Females are browner and young birds have little more than a streak of white in the wing and dull whitish under parts. Their identity can be quite puzzling, but their rich colours, with much orange-brown or reddish, white in the wing (more noticeable in flight), short black legs and ground-loving behaviour (never going into a bush or tree) should help. **Habitat** shingle, sandy beaches with weedy strandline, coastal marshes. **Food** largely seeds. **Voice** includes a loud and sweet *seeu* or *soo*, and a rippling, twittering trill, finishing in a stronger note: *tiririririp.*

Yellowhammer
Emberiza citrinella

Length: 16 cm
2

Weight: 25–30 g
R

The Yellowhammer's most characteristic feature is its lazy, repetitive song, given from a bush in some rough, open place on a hot summer day. Seen well, the male needs little more than its bright yellow head, streaked with black, to identify it. The upper parts are streaked with black and brown, above a chestnut rump; the long tail has white sides, and the underside is yellow, with a chestnut breastband and darker streaks each side. Females are paler but still very yellow birds, and have the same rump and tail colours. Their habit of perching on hedge or bushtops, hopping on the ground on short legs and gathering in flocks in stubbly fields separates Yellowhammers from Yellow Wagtails right away. **Habitat** bushy slopes, rough, gorse-covered ground near the coast, farmland with hedges, commons and heaths; fields and farmyards in winter. **Nest** in the foot of a bush. It lays 3–4 eggs in May; they hatch after 12–14 days and the young fly after 12–13 days. **Food** largely seeds, leaves, buds, grain; also some insects. **Voice** includes a metallic, sharp *twik* or *twilik* in flight. Song is a monotonous but not unpleasant chirping phrase, one note repeated several times, with the last or penultimate one higher and longer— 'a little bit of bread and no cheese'.

Reed Bunting
Emberiza schoeniclus

Length: 15 cm
2

Weight: 16–20 g
R

Widespread, and increasingly seen in drier areas and as a visitor to gardens, the Reed Bunting can be distinguished by its typical bunting build (rather long and slim, with a stout bill, peaky head and short legs) and its overall rufous colour. Males in spring have a black head, with a white moustache and a broad white collar. Otherwise they look rather dark and well-streaked. Females have browner heads, with a pale buff band over the dark ear coverts, and a dark moustache; the rump is brown, the lengthy tail black with broad white sides. The tail is often flicked and jerked open for a moment while the bird is perched. In spring groups of males associate with pipits and wagtails on waterside grassy places. **Habitat** waterside bushes, edges of reed-beds, overgrown ditches and damp bracken slopes. Visits fields in winter. **Nest** in a tussock. The 4–5 eggs hatch after 14 days, and the young leave after 10–13 days. Two broods. **Food** largely seeds and insects. **Voice** is a shrill, but musical *pseu* or *tseep*; song is a short, jangly phrase, such as *tweek tweek tweek tililik*, the first part on one note, the second part quicker and higher.

Corn Bunting
Emberiza calandra

Length: 18 cm
2

Weight: 40–50 g
R

Like the Skylark, the Corn Bunting is of intermediate size—larger than the finches and sparrows, but smaller than the thrushes. That in itself may help to identify it, for otherwise it is fairly nondescript! The general plumage is pale brown above and buff below, all streaked darker. The tail is brown, with no white sides (most buntings show some white); the bill is large, stout and pale. Males, females and young birds are all much alike. The species is unevenly distributed, but is most common in the east. Corn Buntings gather in small flocks, and also join with mixed groups of finches. **Habitat** wide open farmland, especially cereal fields; pastures. **Nest** in thick grass. Lays 3–5 eggs, which hatch after 12–13 days. The young fly after 9–12 days. **Food** largely seeds, fruits, buds and grain; also spiders and insects. **Voice** includes a sharp, abrupt flight note, sounding like *quit* or *plip*. The song is a feature of the open landscape it inhabits, given from an occasional bush or hedge or from ground in the middle of a field; it is a dry, spluttering, short phrase, starting with a few ticking notes and ending in a tinny rattle: *tik tik tik tikiktrree*.

INDEX